ALONE IN THE WORLD

Alone in the World

ORPHANS AND ORPHANAGES IN AMERICA

WITHDRAWN

Catherine Reef

CLARION BOOKS ❧ NEW YORK

Clarion Books
a Houghton Mifflin Company imprint
215 Park Avenue South, New York, NY 10003
Copyright © 2005 by Catherine Reef

The text was set in 13.5-point Galliard.
Book design by Trish Parcell.

www.houghtonmifflinbooks.com

Printed in the U.S.A.

Library of Congress Cataloging-in-Publication Data

Reef, Catherine.

Alone in the world : orphans and orphanages in America / by Catherine Reef.
p. cm.
Includes bibliographical references and index.
ISBN 0-618-35670-3
1. Orphans—United States—History—Juvenile literature.
2. Orphanages—United States—History—Juvenile literature.   I. Title.
HV983.R44   2005
362.730'0973—dc22
2004020179

ISBN-13: 978-0-618-35670-6
ISBN-10: 0-618-35670-3

MP 10 9 8 7 6 5 4 3 2

For my nephews and nieces

CONTENTS

 The Independent Order of Odd Fellows, an organization dedicated to helping people in need, opened orphanages throughout the United States beginning in 1872. This one, in Lincoln, Illinois, was founded in 1893.

CHAPTER 1

THROWN UPON THE WORLD

The Orphan Home, the Orphan Home,
How sweet these words of cheer!
Alone and sad, no more we roam;
Our new bright Home is here.

—Elizabeth G. Barber,
"The Orphans' Welcome," 1855

"Papa, why are we going here? Why can't we stay home with you?" Sammy Arcus tugged at his father's coat, which was wet from the April rain. The rain had soaked Sammy to the skin and turned the road they were walking on to mud.

Sammy was tired. In 1929 it took three hours to travel from the Lower East Side of New York City to the town of Yonkers, New York, seventeen miles away. To a seven-year-old boy the journey seemed endless. First there was a long subway trip from southern Manhattan to the end of the line, Van Cortlandt Park in the Bronx. Then there was a streetcar ride, again to the last stop, in Yonkers. There Sammy, along with his father and nine-year-old brother, Al, set out to walk another two miles to reach their destination, the Hebrew National Orphan Home.

1

Claire Fiance, the social worker who traveled with them, assured Mr. Arcus that the orphanage was not far away now. In Yiddish, a language spoken at the time by many Jews in Europe and the United States, Nathan Arcus told his sons, "Just keep walking."

Two months earlier, life had changed suddenly for Sammy, Al, and their little sister, Henny. That was when their mother, Mollie Arcus, had fallen to her death from the roof of a tenement building. Nathan, an immigrant from Ukraine, had tried since then to keep the family together. But the wages he earned as a garment presser went only so far. How could he pay someone to watch his children all day and still put food on the table? He had no choice but to place them in orphanages. Henny now lived in an asylum that accepted children ages two to five, and Sammy and Al were headed for the home in Yonkers, which was for boys.

At last, there it was: the Hebrew National Orphan Home. The brothers looked up at a massive four-story structure surrounded by a barbed wire–topped fence. They stepped inside. A somber portrait stared down at them from the summit of a wide central staircase. It was of Aaron J. Levy, a

Residents gather in front of the Hebrew National Orphan Home to watch as the American flag is raised on a morning in 1932. Sammy Arcus lived here for eleven years.

justice of the state supreme court and president of the orphanage, dressed in a judge's black robe.

Claire Fiance led the Arcuses to the superintendent's office, and there events happened all too fast. As the boys held on to their father and begged him to take them home, they noticed that he was in tears. Then a man the children had never seen before pulled Al from the room by force. The experience was so traumatic that more than seventy years later, the pain remained fresh in Sam Arcus's memory. "I had lost my mother, I was separated from my baby sister, and some strange man came and took away my brother," he said.

Next, Sammy felt a pair of hands pry him from his father's grasp. They belonged to a blond woman, Mrs. Rubenstein, who supervised the youngest boys. Smiling gently, she led Sammy to the dormitory he would share with fifty to sixty others.

Similar scenes took place throughout the United States in the nineteenth and early twentieth centuries, when children needing society's protection and care typically went to orphan asylums.

Today, when people think about children in orphanages, fictional characters often come to mind. We remember Oliver Twist asking for more food, or Little Orphan Annie singing about tomorrow. We might even imagine ourselves in their place. Who hasn't daydreamed about being alone in the world, living in a gloomy, gray institution, being watched by a heartless matron, and surviving on watery gruel? Who hasn't wondered, Is this how it really was?

It is true that asylums housed "full orphans"—children who had no living parents. More often, though, they cared for "half orphans" like Sammy Arcus—children who had lost a parent to death but still had one living. There were even some poor children with two living parents who spent time in asylums. Their fathers and mothers had no choice but to place the children in orphanages if their families were to survive.

Americans have always found ways to care for poor, orphaned, and abandoned children. In colonial times, people looked after their loved ones and neighbors. There were no big cities or large institutions on American soil, and most colonists lived in small, tightly knit communities. They helped the poor who lived among them and took in boys and girls who had lost their parents. Orphans with no one to raise them became apprentices or indentured servants. They were bound by contract to masters who provided food, clothing, and shelter until the children reached adulthood. An apprentice was likely to be a boy. His master was an artisan who taught him carpentry, blacksmithing, shoemaking, or some other trade. Indentured servants—both girls and boys—were taken in to work rather than learn. These children cooked and cleaned in their masters' homes or labored in their fields.

Of course, it wasn't only orphaned children who worked from an early age. Most children had jobs to do. In colonial America, farming families needed everyone's help to get by. Seven-year-old boys plowed fields, sowed seeds, and weeded vegetable patches. Girls assisted with the many household chores that needed to be done, from churning butter to spinning wool to keeping an eye on younger brothers and sisters. Life was

Everyone in farming families worked hard in the young United States. In this watercolor by the artist John Halkett, painted around 1822, a child learns how to chop wood with an ax.

hard, and children grew up quickly. Most owned just a couple of simple toys and had little time for play.

Society's needs changed around 1820, when factories began drawing people away from farms and into towns and cities. Immigration from northern Europe also caused cities to burgeon. New York City (at that time just Manhattan) was home to about 33,000 people in 1790, according to the U.S. Census Bureau. By 1820, thirty years later, the city's population had risen to 123,700; in another thirty years it more than quadrupled, reaching 515,500.

Many immigrants spent all their money to travel to the United States and arrived with almost nothing. Upon reaching their destination, they competed with American-born workers for low-paying factory work, sometimes without success. Immigrant laborers felt lucky to get jobs building canals or railroads but then found themselves out of work when the project was completed. Job loss, a new baby, illness, or death—anything that upset a family's delicate economic balance—might create a crisis. This was true for immigrants and nonimmigrants alike.

For the first time, well-to-do Americans viewed poverty as a problem. It was hard to ignore the teeming slums just blocks away from bustling business districts and gracious homes. One of the most notorious slums was Five Points, in lower Manhattan, the setting of the 2002 film *Gangs of New York*. There, families lived in squalor in tumbledown houses with sagging roofs, surrounded by saloons and houses of prostitution. Five Points was the scene of constant drunken brawls and was known as a gathering place for criminals. "I would rather risque myself in an Indian fight than venture among these creatures after night," remarked Tennessee congressman Davy Crockett, a veteran of the Indian Wars. Crockett, who toured Five Points in 1834, said, "What a miserable place a city is for poor people: they are half starved, poorly clothed, and perished for fire."

At a time when people burned wood for heat, having firewood could mean the difference between life and death. The price of firewood went up

An early-morning scene in Donovan Lane, near the Five Points section of Manhattan. About twelve hundred boxes of artifacts found in the 1990s at the site of the old Five Points neighborhood were stored in a sub-basement of 6 World Trade Center and lost in the terrorist attack of September 11, 2001. Of 850,000 dishes, pipe fragments, buttons, marbles, and other relics, only eighteen items survive. Artifacts like these provide important clues to how people lived long ago.

during severe winters, and some cities experienced shortages. The poor constantly worried that they might "perish for fire."

The people living in the fine, big houses saw no link between poverty and economic factors, including the low wages that industry paid. Instead, most believed that the poor had only themselves to blame. Poverty, they declared, resulted from weakness and bad habits. Even New Yorker Robert M. Hartley, who formed the New-York Association for Improving the Condition of the Poor, insisted that the needy "are content to live in filth and disorder with a bare subsistence, provided they can drink, and smoke, and gossip. . . ." The offspring of the poor, said New York City's chief of police, are "the vagrant and vicious children, of both sexes, who infest our public thoroughfares, hotels, docks, &c.—who are . . . only destined to a life of misery, shame, and crime. . . ." (To Americans of the time, a vicious person was someone addicted to harmful habits and immoral behavior.)

Local governments, churches, and charities helped the poor by giving them food, firewood, or small sums of money. But with more and more families living in poverty, this kind of aid grew costly. Some towns and cities spent more on relief for the poor than on building schools, paving roads, or anything else. There was also the worry that giving the poor something for nothing might destroy their desire to work. It was the opinion of a Pennsylvania writer in 1827 that when the jobless poor were given handouts, "They are not left to feel the just consequences of their own idleness." Even more damage was done, he said, because "The industrious poor are discouraged, by observing the bounty bestowed upon the idle, which they can only obtain by the sweat of their brow."

The solution in many places was the poorhouse, also called almshouse, an institution to shelter the poor and teach them good work habits. The poorhouse served, too, as a storage place for orphaned or abandoned children. Poorhouses could be large or small. Those in cities often resembled the Boston House of Industry, where men and women slept separately in

Two brothers and a sister use their pennies to buy bread for a hungry beggar boy in an American children's book from 1817.

two large wings, while those in rural areas were likely to be abandoned farmhouses. Poorhouses quickly increased in number. Massachusetts had 83 in 1824 and 219 by 1860. Maryland in 1860 had almshouses in every county but one, and they were common in other states as well.

Almshouse managers expected most able-bodied inmates to work in order to pay for their support. Women sewed, spun thread, or nursed the sick, and men performed tasks that benefited the community, perhaps farming or repairing roads. Some almshouses were called workhouses, and in these inmates labored at jobs that no one else wanted to do, such as picking oakum. The workers tore up their fingers as they picked apart old ropes, creating loose piles of fiber, or oakum. The community then sold the oakum to shipbuilders, who mixed it with tar to make a thick, sticky substance for sealing the hulls of ships.

Some almshouses were clean and orderly, but most were filthy, dangerous places where all kinds of people, young and old, lived packed together. A typical poorhouse was the Commercial Hospital in Cincinnati, Ohio, which opened in 1821. This institution contained 150 beds for the sick and 34 cells where mentally ill people were chained to the floor. Most of the poor slept in the building's upper stories, but children slept in the basement with the old and the blind. Food was both meager and bad, to hold costs down, keep life from becoming too comfortable, and encourage the poor to support themselves.

Things were no better in New York than in Ohio. A committee appointed by the New York State Senate to investigate almshouses reported in 1857: "The poor houses throughout the State may generally be described as badly constructed, ill-arranged, ill-warmed, and ill-ventilated. The rooms are crowded with inmates; and the air, particularly in the sleeping apartments, is very noxious. . . ." In the town of Clinton, New York, poorhouse inmates consumed nothing but pea soup and dirty water. "Common domestic animals are usually more humanely provided for than the paupers in these institutions," the committee concluded.

Diseases spread readily in these foul places. If one badly nourished almshouse child picked up an infection, others soon had it, too. In 1831 many of the seven hundred children in New York City's Bellevue Almshouse had ophthalmia, a severe eye infection that can damage the inner structures of the eye. The city hired a doctor to treat the children, but ophthalmia remained a problem in the almshouse a year later.

"The poorhouse became the dumping-ground for the wreckage and waste of human society," said Homer Folks, a pioneering social worker, in the late 1800s. Every day, children in almshouses came in contact with

The Philadelphia almshouse as it looked in 1799. A high wall fenced in the city's poor.

murderers, thieves, prostitutes, the sick, and the dying. Concerned citizens asked, How can we separate these children from evil influences and prevent them from developing the bad habits that lead to poverty? The answer seemed to lie in another type of institution: the orphan asylum.

There had been homes for orphans in North America since 1729. In that year Roman Catholic nuns in New Orleans opened a school and hospital to care for girls orphaned in Indian attacks. But by 1800 there were still only seven orphan asylums, at most, in the United States. They became more common after 1830, as the number of children needing care increased.

The asylum was to be a haven, a place where children could live in safety and be fed, clothed, and taught. "Shelter Us Under the Shadow of Thy Wings" was carved in the cornerstone of a home for Jewish orphans, the Hebrew Sheltering Guardian Society of New York City.

Some asylums were founded to house children orphaned by epidemics of yellow fever and other diseases. Every summer, mosquitoes brought yellow fever to the steamy South. Following the summer of 1817, when yellow fever struck New Orleans especially hard, a group of Protestant women in that city founded the Poydras Asylum, a home for girls who had lost their parents in the epidemic. The asylum was named for Julien de Lallande Poydras, the Louisiana politician whose money supported it.

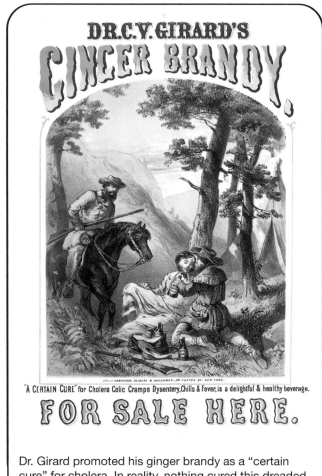

Dr. Girard promoted his ginger brandy as a "certain cure" for cholera. In reality, nothing cured this dreaded disease.

In cities, where sewage regularly contaminated the water supply, cholera and typhus spread rapidly, causing numerous deaths and leaving children in need of care. A cholera epidemic that moved through the United States in 1832 killed thousands of people and orphaned many children. The epidemic reached Cincinnati in October. On a single day, October 21, forty-one city residents died. In all, Cincinnati lost more than five hundred people to cholera in 1832. "The din of the city was hushed," wrote one witness, "and every day appeared as Sunday. For weeks funeral processions might be seen at all hours, from early morning to late at night."

On January 25, 1833, almost as soon as the epidemic waned, city residents opened an orphan asylum to take in the children who had been left in need. Local merchants donated buttons, cloth, and hats to dress the orphans, and blankets to keep them warm at night. Volunteers in the community knitted stockings and sewed clothing by hand.

Wars created orphans, too. Well-meaning men and women in Philadelphia and other cities opened orphanages following the War of 1812. In 1815 several "well-placed and elegant ladies" in the nation's capital founded the Washington City Orphan Asylum to house local girls orphaned by the war. The number of Americans who died in combat in the War of 1812 was relatively small—2,260—although the number of soldiers who died of other causes, such as disease, is unknown. Because many more soldiers died from disease than from battle wounds in other nineteenth-century wars, it is likely that the same was true in the War of 1812.

By 1860 there were 124 orphan asylums in the United States. By 1888 there were 613, housing more than fifty thousand children. These youngsters were "little ones who seem to have been thrown upon a loveless world," said one Chicago minister. Most asylums were run by religious or charitable groups for children of one faith or another. And most of the people who oversaw the daily operation of asylums were women, including Roman Catholic nuns.

Asylums offered women a chance to work and help society at a time when many careers were closed to them. Some of the staff lived in the asylum and put in long days caring for the orphans. They had little time to rest, because there was always a child who needed something.

The asylum was to be a home, and the matron, or female head of that home, was to be like a mother to the orphans, providing tenderness and comfort. It was her duty to "instill into the youthful minds around her, feelings of reverence and gratitude to their Heavenly Father and to impress upon them a sense of their moral responsibilities, and the lessons of virtue and piety," said the managers of the Orphan House of Charleston, South Carolina. Americans commonly believed that women were nurturers, while it was the men who had a head for business. That's why men controlled the budget and paid the bills at nearly every asylum in the first half of the nineteenth century. Women managers did have a voice in some policy deci-

Flames destroy the U.S. Capitol as British forces capture Washington, D.C., in 1814. In the War of 1812 the British burned the Capitol, the White House, other government buildings, and surrounding homes, leaving children in need of shelter.

sions, such as which children to accept and whether to allow parents to visit.

Some of the Protestant, Catholic, and Jewish asylums in the United States took only girls; some took only boys; and others accepted children of both sexes. Asylums discriminated by race, with nearly all accepting white children only.

Until 1865 most of the black children in the United States lived in slavery. Some enslaved children lost parents through death, but many were separated from their parents when someone in the family was sold. Ordinarily, other slaves informally adopted children whose parents had died or been sold. They also adopted children who were newly purchased and arrived on the plantation knowing no one.

Informal adoptions took place as well among free African Americans, but many free black orphans begged on street corners, swept chimneys, or did other grimy work. Denied admittance to most poorhouses, they sometimes slept in jails. A number of private citizens opened orphanages for African Americans in the nineteenth century. The first was the New York Colored Orphan Asylum, which was founded by Quakers in Manhattan in 1836.

Even a three-story brick structure could not protect the orphans from racial hatred, however. On July 13, 1863, a white mob broke down the door of the Colored Orphan Asylum and set the building on fire. This happened during the Civil War, when the United States, in need of soldiers, began issuing draft notices. Being forced to fight a war to free African-American slaves angered some white northerners. Foreign-born laborers especially feared competition for jobs from the freed slaves. For four days in the summer of 1863, enraged whites rioted in New York City. They burned not only the Colored Orphan Asylum but also the homes and businesses of African Americans. The orphans escaped to safety through the asylum's side door and found temporary shelter in a police station and an asylum for white children. In 1867 the Quakers rebuilt the home on 143rd Street, in northern Manhattan. The asylum later moved outside the city, to the suburb of Riverdale.

In 1855 Quakers also founded the Thomas Asylum for Orphan and Destitute Indian Children. This orphanage sheltered Seneca Indian children whose parents had died of starvation or disease after being forced to give up hunting and move to the Cattaraugus Indian Reservation in western New York. The Thomas Asylum took in orphaned and needy Indian children living throughout New York State as well.

The Thomas Asylum, like the Poydras Asylum, the Washington City Orphan Asylum, and most orphanages, now belongs to history. Today the poor receive public assistance in the form of money and social services intended to keep families together. Government aid takes many forms, from federally funded food stamps to state-sponsored Medicaid, a program designed to provide medical care to the poor. It varies from job training for adults to Head Start, preschool classes that prepare children for kindergarten.

A mob burns and loots the New York Colored Orphan Asylum while children run to safety.

A small number of children's homes still operate in the United States, but most are called residential or congregate-care facilities, or group homes. Many house children with special needs. Young people whose relatives cannot take care of them usually live with foster or adoptive families. Traditional orphanages have come to seem stern, cold, and cruel.

The knowledge of orphan asylums that we have today has been gathered by historians who have combed through old letters, record books, photographs, and other evidence. Most of the historical documents relating to orphanages were written by asylum managers and other adult observers. Historical accounts written by orphans themselves are rare. Very few of the thousands of American children who spent time within asylum walls left written records of their experiences. It may be that they preferred to forget the orphanage, or perhaps they went on to lead hard lives and had little time to reflect or write.

Sam Arcus at about the age of sixteen, in a photograph taken at the Hebrew National Orphan Home.

Sam Arcus is one of the exceptions. He has lived a full life and has enjoyed a long career as a social worker. He also has written memoirs and short stories based on his years at the Hebrew National Orphan Home. He never has forgotten his first day at the orphanage, a day spent learning to do what the other boys did and trying to catch sight of his brother.

The first night, lying on his iron cot in a room full of sleeping boys, Sammy Arcus believed he had been abandoned. "When the lights are out, you feel alone," he later said. "That is when I really cried."

Mrs. Rubenstein heard Sammy's sobs and spoke words of comfort. "Yes, yes, it's very hard," he recalled her saying. "You will get used to it in time.

 Marcia Burnes Van Ness, second lady manager of the Washington City Orphan Asylum, typified the kind and tender matron. The wife of a politician, she devoted her time to charitable work. When Van Ness died in 1832 the sculptor and poet Horatio Greenough wrote:

> 'Mid rank and wealth and worldly pride,
> From every snare she turned aside.
> She sought the low, the humble shed,
> Where gaunt disease and famine tread. . . .

ASYLUM CHILDREN

I am a little orphan, but pleasant are my days,
For on my lonely pathway, God sheds His kindest rays;
My life so calm and happy, so bright and active is,
There's scarce a joy I wish for to crown my earthly bliss.

—Anonymous, "I Am a Little Orphan," 1847

Through much of the nineteenth century, orphanages broke families apart. A parent placing a child in an asylum usually was forced to give up all rights to him or her. Many asylum managers believed that separating children from their parents once and for all was in the children's best interest. They knew of no better way to prevent the children from learning bad habits, like drunkenness and laziness, that might lead them into poverty.

Throughout the United States destitute parents agreed in writing not to interfere in the raising of their sons and daughters. This was a very hard step to take. These parents knew they would never again comfort their children in sickness; they would never again watch their children play or share their joy. They were to have no say in what their children learned in

Washington, April 21st 1828

This is to certify that I freely ~~& willingly~~ relinquish ~~Jeanna & Eliza Ann Henley~~ Eliza Ann ~~Henley~~ & Joanna Henley my children to the Managers of the Orphan Asylum, ~~and~~ and I promise to contribute $1 per month towards their support.

Witness

Mary W Jackson

Deborah + Henley
her   mark

By making her mark on this document, a woman named Deborah Henley signed over custody of her two daughters, Eliza Ann and Joanna, to the managers of the Washington City Orphan Asylum on April 21, 1828. She also promised to pay one dollar each month toward the cost of her children's support. Mrs. Henley signed with a cross because she was illiterate.

school, how they were taught to worship, or how they were disciplined. Many mothers and fathers, unable to read or write, signed away their parental rights by making a mark on a printed surrender form.

Some asylum managers had a bit more respect for family ties among the poor. The managers of the Chicago Orphan Asylum, for example, allowed parents to leave their children for three months. At the end of that period, mothers and fathers who could provide a stable home were permitted to take their children back, while those who could not provide a home lost their rights. A small number of asylums let parents retain their rights indefinitely. These were places like St. Mary's Female Asylum, founded in Cleveland, Ohio, in 1851, which cared for girls only until their families' troubles eased. A few orphanages let parents visit their children at scheduled times—for example, on the last Saturday of each month. At the New York Juvenile Asylum a committee decided whether parents might visit their children, and when.

Coming to an orphanage was tough on everyone in a family. Parents and children alike felt the pain of separation, but usually there was nothing else to be done. Often a family's hardship began when the father died of illness or from an accident on the job. Because working people rarely had savings or life insurance, surviving family members would be plunged into poverty. It was possible, too, that a widowed mother needed to work and had no one to watch her children.

Asylums took in children like John Dieter of New Orleans, who was nine years old in 1835, when

Authorities found these children living in a Washington, D.C., alley with their widowed, alcohol-dependent mother. The hungry, neglected children entered the Washington City Orphan Asylum, and their mother was sent to the poorhouse.

Almshouse managers commonly placed abandoned infants with wet nurses, who were women hired to nurse them. Each wet nurse was permitted to have one breastfeeding baby and two others who had been weaned. Some of these women were cruel and dishonest. In 1859 New York City police officers investigating a robbery found three starving infants in the care of this woman, Mrs. Carlock. An almshouse had been paying Mrs. Carlock one dollar a week to care for the children, and a doctor had certified that she had "a fresh breast of milk."

his widowed, ill father brought him to the Asylum for Destitute Orphan Boys. They took in children like three-day-old Samuel, last name unknown, whose desperate mother left him on the steps of a Washington, D.C., orphanage on Tuesday, March 6, 1832. Occasionally, children brought themselves to institutions. In 1853 eleven-year-old Mary Ann Croghan knocked on the door of the Charleston, South Carolina, poorhouse, wanting to escape the constant drinking and fighting that went on in her home. The poorhouse steward turned Mary Ann over to the city orphanage.

There were a great many children needing care, and asylums had only so much room. For this reason asylum managers would not take just any child. Children had to be healthy to enter an orphanage, although malnutrition, lice, and the mites that cause scabies, an itchy rash, were allowed. Children who were sick or hard to discipline were rejected. Asylums also set age limits: Many turned away children older than ten or twelve, who were considered old enough to work. Most refused to take children younger than three, since babies and toddlers were more likely than older children to die from disease. (In fact, the infant named Samuel died in August 1832, at five months of age.)

Babies entrusted to Sister Irene at the New York Foundling Hospital had a better chance of survival than those given to wet nurses. Yet even with the best care, small children in institutions died at alarming rates. The New York Foundling Hospital was one of the few nineteenth-century orphanages that accepted infants. A mother was permitted to stay at the home and breastfeed her baby if she would feed another infant as well.

It was not uncommon for children of all ages to die of scarlet fever, measles, whooping cough, or some other disease, no matter where they lived. Asylums had an especially high death rate, because contagious diseases spread rapidly when many children lived together. In 1849 twenty children died at the Colored Orphan Asylum in New York City, nine of them from cholera.

In 1840 the managers of the Washington City Orphan Asylum were pleased to report, "within the last twelve months the withering hand of sickness has but barely touched the inmates of the Orphan's home: One infant spirit has been translated to a brighter world." One or two deaths in a year was a statistic worthy of pride.

Crude living conditions in many asylums promoted the spread of disease. It was not unusual, in the first half of the nineteenth century, for orphans to sleep three or four to a bed. They bathed rarely and wore grimy, stained clothes, giving asylums the sour "poor-house smell" that anyone who

Residents, staff, and directors pose outside the Christian Orphans' Home of Holdrege, Nebraska. The home accepted children from all over the United States.

worked among the needy knew all too well. In 1859, when four Roman Catholic nuns took charge of St. Vincent's Orphan Asylum in Philadelphia, they found that of the twenty-seven children in the orphanage, "thirteen were suffering from a skin disease over the whole body. . . . The children had no clothes for a change, only one suit which they wore. In school there were only three decent school benches; in the parlor, four simple green chairs; rough boards served as tables in the kitchen."

Children at the Charleston Orphan House spent the night on wooden cots infested with bedbugs. These flat, brown insects feed at night on the blood of sleeping hosts, leaving itchy welts. The asylum finally replaced the cots with iron beds, which offered bedbugs fewer hiding places, around 1855.

As illnesses raged and subsided, and children died or recovered, asylum life went on. Newcomers quickly learned that a day in an orphanage was governed by the clock. Orphans followed a strict schedule, going from one task to another at specified times. They woke up, dressed, ate, prayed, and had their lessons at the same times every day. "Everything moves by machinery," observed the writer Lydia Maria Child, who visited a Long Island, New York, asylum in the 1840s.

Girls at the Boston Female Asylum in the early nineteenth century followed a typical schedule. They woke up at six A.M. from April through October. They slept a little later—until seven A.M.—for the rest of the year. The first thing they did upon waking was pray. Then they washed their faces in cold water and cleaned their sleeping quarters before reporting for breakfast at eight o'clock. At nine they read from the Bible, prayed again, and began their school day. At one P.M. the girls ate dinner, the main meal of the day. School resumed at two and lasted until five, when the girls were allowed an hour of play before supper. They went to bed at eight, after saying still more prayers.

According to the constitution of the Female Orphan Asylum of Portland, Maine, which was established in 1828, "From the first of April

Inside the Christian Orphans' Home at Holdrege: dormitories, a large hall, the schoolroom, the dining hall, and the parlor. These images may have been used to raise funds.

to the first of October, the Children shall rise at six o'clock, say their Prayers, wash themselves, comb their hair, make their beds, and clean their chambers; breakfast at seven; play or work in the garden until nine, when the governess shall read a chapter in the Bible and pray with them; attend school until twelve, dine at one, play until two, attend school until five, after which, play one hour. In the evening say their Prayers, go to bed at eight, wash their feet every night." During the rest of the year, when days were shorter, the girls rose at seven A.M., went to bed at seven P.M., and washed their feet just once a week. "The children shall be dressed in a plain manner and treated with kindness," said the founders of this institution.

Managers sought to provide the children not just with a home, food, and clothing, but with education and moral and religious training as well. Prayer and Bible study were strong medicine meant to protect the children from the sinfulness of poverty. "Each day shall begin and end with worship" was the rule at the Protestant Orphan Asylum of Cleveland, Ohio, and at many other institutions.

Silence during meals was another common rule. The children had to eat their meals without saying a word to their neighbors. Orphans of the early 1800s ate a monotonous diet that rarely included fresh fruits and vegetables. Records from the Cincinnati Orphan Asylum suggest that the children living there in the 1830s ate bread and molasses, drank water or weak coffee, and had little else.

Orphans fared slightly better at the Boston Female Asylum. Breakfast for them was rice with molasses or milk, porridge, or hasty pudding, which is a boiled custard made with flour or cornmeal. On Mondays and Wednesdays the girls had soup for their main meal. They ate boiled meat on Tuesdays, sometimes with vegetables but more often without. They sat down to beans or peas with pork on Thursdays, broth on Fridays, and fish on Saturdays. On Sundays the girls enjoyed roasted meat and pudding. (In the 1800s a pudding served with dinner was not sweet. Its main ingredient might have been stale bread or suet.)

Most mornings the Female Orphan Asylum of Portland served porridge or bread with milk for breakfast. Dinner was fresh or salted meat, fresh or salted fish, or dried beans or peas, and possibly vegetables or pudding. Supper, the light evening meal, was usually bread, hasty pudding, or rice with milk.

Meals at the New York Foundling Hospital were quiet, orderly events.

An orphanage might have been located in the heart of an American city, but the children inside lived apart from the world around them. The orphanage became home, school, and church, and the boys and girls who lived there rarely ventured beyond its confines. The outside community called them asylum children.

Schooling took place inside the asylum. Public-school systems were small and new, and they had no room for all the poor children living nearby. For a long time no one in the United States had to go to school. There were no laws requiring children to attend school until 1850, when

Massachusetts passed the first compulsory-education law. Most other states passed similar laws much later, between 1870 and 1900.

What was school in an orphanage like? A committee investigating the Orphan House of Charleston in 1850 concluded that the orphans' education "might be better." With seventy-three pupils studying under one teacher, the schoolroom was a noisy, chaotic place. Children scribbled curse words on the walls and relieved themselves in the corners. Conditions improved five years later, when the asylum added six teachers to its staff and divided the children into classes according to age and ability. Yet the orphans still learned by rote—by memorizing lessons—as pupils did in most U.S. schools at the time.

Orphans clearly benefited from the education they received, regardless of its quality. Of the twenty-five children who entered the Cincinnati Orphan Asylum when it opened in 1833, only two or three knew how to read. At the end of one year, the managers reported: "There are now five classes—the youngest, (children four or five years old) who spell words of one syllable; the intermediate classes still further advanced; and a class of the oldest children, who read in the [Bible] with ease, are learning to write, and have some knowledge of the rudiments of arithmetic."

The Orphans' Home and Asylum, an Episcopal orphanage in New York City, offered a typical course of study. Children living there in the 1850s learned "reading, writing, spelling, geography, arithmetic, and Church Catechism." The managers of this institution wanted to mold the children into adults "having all the characteristics of the useful member of society— healthy in body, healthy in mind, and, above all, healthy in soul."

When they were not in school, at meals, or at prayer, asylum children had chores to do. They swept floors, dusted furniture, made beds, helped in the kitchen, and washed and mended clothes. The children's labor saved the asylum money; instead of paying wages to maids, the managers had more to spend on food and other necessities. The managers of the Washington City Orphan Asylum noted in 1861:

We have recently been able to dispense with the services of the cook, nurse, & seamstress as several of the girls are now able to undertake those departments under the supervision of the matron. Very excellent bread is made by the young cook, the little children are affectionately attended to by the older ones—a portion of the needlework & cutting of garments is accomplished by them; & this year's supply of stockings has been knit by seven or eight girls. Thus we hope to train their hearts & hands for positions of usefulness & trust.

There were also moral reasons for requiring the asylum children to perform chores. Like the Puritans who settled in New England in the 1600s, Americans of the nineteenth century equated work with virtue and godliness. They thought that work taught children self-control and prepared them for later life. Many Americans still feel this way.

American children of the early 1800s sat through frequent lessons in moral behavior. One children's picture book from this period was filled with wisdom like the following: "Many have been the boys who have fallen victim to disobedience and rashness. Indeed, bad children must not think that their punishment will always be put off till after death." The book also taught its young readers this lesson: "The first symptom of real grief is remorse, or a painful recollection that we have done wrong."

Keeping children busy with brooms and dust cloths prevented them from getting into trouble—or so many people believed. There were always orphans who broke the rules, who whispered during dinner or spoke rudely to an adult. These children received spankings or other punishments. They might be assigned extra chores, sent to bed without supper, made to feel ashamed, or placed in solitary confinement. Punishments could seem cruel by twenty-first-century standards. For example, one boy who talked back to the matron of a Charleston, South Carolina, asylum spent several days locked in a cellar, living on bread and water, until he apologized.

Even children who obeyed the rules and escaped punishment by adults

Whatever your diversions are,
Pursue them all with proper care,
And never, till your task is done,
To any play attempt to run.

Moral Recreations, in Prose and Verse, a children's book published in 1800, advises readers to use care and caution while playing. It warns that even a game of leapfrog can be dangerous.

suffered at the hands of older boys and girls. Bullying was part of everyday life in an asylum, as older orphans brutalized younger ones and took new-comers' possessions. And, most likely, some children were sexually abused by older residents and staff members. Sexual abuse occurred at orphanages in the twentieth century, and nineteenth-century asylums were not any safer.

Fortunately, orphanages were meant to be temporary homes. Most orphans spent one to four years in an asylum, although a number stayed five years or longer. Some parents who still had rights to their children eventually reclaimed them, and a few girls and boys ran away. But children who were full orphans or whose parents had surrendered their rights—in other words, most asylum residents—were placed in new homes whenever possible.

A small number of asylum children went to new homes because they were adopted, but many more were indentured. The managers of the Washington City Orphan Asylum wanted to see children "placed in a situation where every effort will be made so to inform their minds, and mold their characters that they may be useful members of society while they remain on Earth." Other asylum managers had similar ideas. John Dieter, the nine-year-old whose sick father gave him up in 1835, spent four years in the Asylum for Destitute Orphan Boys. While he was there, his father died, leaving John a full orphan. John was indentured to a sea captain and embarked on a maritime career.

Asylum managers were often careless when investigating homes for indentured youth, if they investigated at all. They easily accepted recommendations from clergymen and friends, at times with distressing results. Some indentured children were neglected or overworked, and some were sent back to asylums because of bad behavior. In the 1840s the managers of a New Haven, Connecticut, orphan asylum tried ten times to place one girl as a servant, and each time she was returned. The women managers prayed with the girl and pleaded with her to change her ways, but their words had little effect.

Gradually, states passed laws to protect the rights of indentured youth. An 1845 Illinois law permitted an orphan asylum to bind a child younger than fourteen into indenture as a clerk, apprentice, or servant without the child's consent. As a result, even babies were bound by contract to grow up in their master's home and start working as soon as they were big enough. Children age fourteen or older had to agree to be indentured. By law, an indentured white child was to learn reading, writing, basic arithmetic, and a job skill that was useful to the community. (A black child did not have to be taught reading, writing, or arithmetic until the law was revised in 1874.)

When the period of indenture ended—at age eighteen for girls and twenty-one for boys—the master was to provide the young person with a Bible and two changes of clothing "suitable to his or her condition in life." It was up to the asylum manager and a judge of the state court "to see that the terms of such indentures are complied with, and that such minor is not ill used." Whether managers and judges carried out this duty is unknown. The only proof that negligent masters were made to comply with the law would lie in the court record, and no cases of this nature came to trial in Illinois in the nineteenth century.

 The boys' cell in Manhattan's Halls of Justice,
a jail known popularly as the Tombs.

SAVING YOUTHFUL HEARTS

Some of them merest children yet,
With no home but the street,
Just such ones you have often met,
With shoeless feet . . .
And others older,
With bearing bolder,
On whose features the seal of vice is set.

—ANONYMOUS, "THE BOYS' CELL," 1870

Nineteenth-century Americans hoped that asylums would prevent needy children from acquiring the "vicious tempers and habits" that led to poverty and crime. What was to be done, though, with young people who had already picked up wicked ways? Juvenile delinquency, like poverty, was a growing problem in the early 1800s. Each year as many as two hundred children between the ages of seven and fourteen appeared in court in New York City alone. Because Americans commonly believed that upon reaching the age of seven a child could tell right from wrong, the courts treated these young people like adults.

This meant that children who were found guilty went to prison with hardened criminals. The Reverend John Stanford, chaplain of the city's

"The Bad Husband": The family in this Currier & Ives print is poor and homeless as a result of the father's laziness and drinking. According to popular opinion, the children were at risk of learning his bad habits and entering into a life of crime. Prints sold by the firm of Currier & Ives decorated many nineteenth-century American homes. They depicted all kinds of things: battles, ships at sea, portraits of presidents, and scenes of country life.

prisons, called the adult inmates "crocodiles in human shape." To him they were cunning creatures who gained the children's trust only to teach them how to be better pickpockets and thieves. "With extended jaws they lay in wait to catch the young offender," Stanford wrote. He asked, "What generous soul but shudders on beholding scenes like these, and ardently wishes to rescue such young delinquents from the jaws of total destruction!"

The situation was harmful to the youngsters and dangerous for society, because children schooled by adults behind bars often grew up to be career criminals. "Many notorious thieves infesting the city were at first idle, vagrant boys, *imprisoned for a short period to keep them from mischief,*" observed Hugh Maxwell, New York City district attorney, in 1822.

Some juries refused to convict children. As a result, there were youngsters who appeared in court again and again to face charges of petty theft, only to return to the streets each time.

Americans of the nineteenth century attacked social problems by forming societies and building institutions. They founded groups such as the Philadelphia Society for Alleviating the Miseries of the Public Prisons and the Society for the Encouragement of Faithful Domestic Servants. They built lunatic asylums, Sunday schools for the children of factory workers, public schools, and, of course, almshouses and orphan asylums.

Another kind of institution, the house of refuge, allowed children convicted of crimes to serve their sentences apart from adults and, it was hoped, learn the errors of their ways. The first such place in the United States, the New York House of Refuge, began operation on January 1, 1825, in a building that had been used by the army to store guns and ammunition.

The New York House of Refuge had been started by a charitable group, the Society for the Reformation of Juvenile Delinquents, but it was supervised by the state and, after 1829, supported by taxes. In this institution, said one of its founders, "Unless the heart is corrupt indeed, and sunk deep in guilt, the youth would undergo a change of feeling and character, and he would look on crime with greater abhorrence."

Just nine months after the House of Refuge opened, District Attorney Maxwell reported optimistically, "The most depraved boys have been withdrawn from the haunts of vice, and the examples which they gave in a great degree destroyed. . . . Of this I am certain, that no institution has ever been formed in this country by benevolent men, more useful or beneficent."

When the inmates moved into a new building, on Christmas Day 1825,

The Harlem River separated New York's House of Refuge from Manhattan. The House of Refuge moved to this location in 1854.

the Reverend John Stanford told them to regard it as a "hospitable dwelling, in which you enjoy comfort, and safety from those who once led you astray." And, he added, "this is the best home many of you ever enjoyed!"

Other cities soon followed New York's example. Philadelphia's house of refuge opened in 1826, and Boston's in 1828. Construction of the Baltimore House of Refuge began in 1851. During the ceremony to mark the laying of its cornerstone, a prominent businessman said, "We would take the pliant spirit of youth and gain to it virtue. . . . We would save the youthful heart from hardening into the rigid and miserable bias of crime." By 1860 there were approximately sixty houses of refuge operating or being built in about twenty cities.

In 1842 the English writer Charles Dickens visited the House of Reformation for Juvenile Offenders in Boston. Dickens, author of *Oliver Twist* and other novels about mistreated orphans and sinister institutions, watched the boys at work. They were making baskets and palm-leaf hats. He also observed their school and listened as they sang a song in celebration of liberty. It was "an odd, and, one would think, rather aggravating theme for prisoners," Dickens said. Although he saw few pleasant expressions on the inmates' faces, Dickens praised the institution's mission, which was "to reclaim the youthful criminal by firm, but kind and judicious, treatment. . . . To snatch him from destruction and restore him to society a penitent and useful member."

Houses of refuge accepted children who had been convicted of crimes or found living on the street by police. Like orphan asylums, they also sheltered poor children whose parents could not afford their care. Now and then, fathers and mothers brought in sons or daughters who were impossi-

* New York City's commissioners of charity question children picked up by the police for peddling or engaging in suspicious activities. Some of these children will be sent to the House of Refuge.

ble to manage at home. Of the sixteen children who entered the New York House of Refuge when it opened in 1825, only seven had actually broken the law.

Unlike orphan asylums, most houses of refuge sheltered both white and black children—but they maintained strict segregation within their walls. "It was painful to observe the studied manner in which the white and colored children were separated and distinguished from each other," noted Edward Strutt Abdy, a British writer who toured the United States in the 1830s. Abdy failed to see the benefit of teaching white children to be proud of their race and blacks to be ashamed of theirs. In 1849 Philadelphians took segregation a step further by opening the House of Refuge for Colored Juvenile Delinquents, an institution exclusively for African Americans.

White or black, young people confined to houses of refuge worked, and worked hard. Work was the cure for delinquency, according to the founders and managers of these homes. Generally, boys did manufacturing work, while girls acquired housekeeping skills that would equip them to be servants later on. Boys at the New York House of Refuge made shoes and men's suits. In other institutions boys caned furniture or made umbrellas, brooms, or nails. Girls washed and mended clothes, made beds, cooked, and scrubbed floors. The youngest children at the Philadelphia House of Refuge did a job requiring less skill: picking burrs from newly shorn wool.

Some inmates worked for part of the day in factories for employers who had contracted with the house of refuge for labor. This practice was gradually phased out, however. It quickly brought complaints from labor unions that the children, who worked without pay, took jobs away from wage-earning adults. And some parents complained that their children were being made to do unskilled factory work and not being taught useful trades. The contract system also put children at risk. In July 1826 a shoe manufacturer was accused of committing the "heinous crime of seduction," or sexually abusing two girls who had come to work for him from the New York House of Refuge. Following a brief investigation, the house of refuge ended its partnership with the shoemaker.

At the New York House of Refuge the children's workday began well before sunrise, when a clanging bell jarred them awake. They had fifteen minutes to dress before the bell rang again, signaling the staff to unlock the cells where the children slept. Each windowless cell measured eight feet long and five feet wide and was furnished with only a cot. "It would be no great piece of extravagance, if every cell contained a shelf or table which might suffice to write upon or hold books," noted Elijah Devoe, an assistant superintendent of the New York House of Refuge, but there were no shelves or tables. "Each room should also be provided with a cup, that might be filled with drinking water," Devoe wrote. Devoe was fired in 1848 following a dispute with his boss and wrote a book exposing what he saw as flaws of the house of refuge.

After marching to the washroom and then lining up for inspection, the boys and girls marched to the chapel to pray. They then spent an hour in school, learning to read, write, spell, and do arithmetic in a room that was stuffy in winter and hot in summer. At seven A.M. a bell signaled that it was time for breakfast.

Another bell at seven-thirty meant that it was time to start work. The children worked steadily until noon, when the bell rang for dinner, a meal that often included beef. The meat was tough, but it was filling and nutritious. Because talking during meals was forbidden, the inmates used signals to communicate their needs. They held up a hand to ask for water and a thumb for vinegar. Three raised fingers meant "bread," and one meant "salt." At one o'clock the children were back at work. They had to wait until five o'clock for the bell that announced quitting time. Then there was another march to the washroom before supper, the worst meal of the day. The cornmeal mush served in the evenings was watery and slimy because it was always undercooked. It was very difficult to properly boil a large amount of mush in the steam-heated cauldrons that the cooks used. The

At the Western House of Refuge in Rochester, New York, a wall divided the yard to keep young boys away from older inmates more experienced in crime.

mush was so bad that about half the children left it untouched. "Some complain that it is too relaxing to the bowels; others find it so unpalatable that they cannot eat it," wrote Elijah Devoe.

Following supper, the exhausted children spent two and a half additional hours at school. At last, they said their evening prayers and marched back to their cells, to be locked up like the prisoners that they were. On hot nights some children slept on the floor, trying to suck fresh air from beneath their doors.

Inmates who broke the rules were punished like prisoners. They were shackled in chains attached to heavy iron balls, placed in handcuffs and leg irons, fed laxatives, or held in solitary confinement. They were whipped or thrashed with strips of rattan on the palms of their hands, the soles of their feet, and other parts of their bodies. "I asked an intelligent boy who had been several years in the House, what were the most disagreeable things in the Refuge," wrote Elijah Devoe. "'After the cat [whip] and rattan,' said he, 'cold cells in winter, hot cells in summer, and bed bugs.'"

On January 28, 1825, Joseph Curtis, the first superintendent of the New York House of Refuge, punished two girls who talked during a meal by tying their hands and feet to a barrel and whipping their bare buttocks. On March 1, 1825, and again on March 18, Curtis whipped one small boy for wetting his bed. On March 13 he placed leg irons on a girl who "does not obey the orders for coming when called and neglects her work for play in the yard."

It is surprising to note that Curtis is the same man who made this statement: "I do not believe that the mind of a human being can be brought to that quiet and progressive state of respect for himself and others while the body is suffering punishment." In fact, his employers considered him too lenient, especially with children who tried to escape, and they fired him in 1826. Curtis felt a bond of affection for the House of Refuge and its inmates, though. For the rest of his life, he visited on Sunday afternoons to lecture the children. He also bequeathed his portrait to the institution, where it hung for years. "To this day," wrote Bradford K. Peirce, chaplain of the New York House of Refuge, in 1869, "that face, hanging upon the wall of the superintendent's office, glances down . . . upon every new-comer as he enters the institution, and upon the discharged child as he receives his farewell counsels, and goes out again into a life of temptation."

Most houses of refuge graded inmates' behavior to determine who would receive privileges and who would be deprived. The managers of the Philadelphia House of Refuge devised four classifications. Class I contained "the best behaved . . . those who do not swear, lie, or use profane, obscene or indecent language or conversation, who attend to their work and studies, are not quarrelsome and have not attempted to escape." In contrast, Class IV was for children who were "very vicious and disobedient." In some institutions boys and girls wore badges on their sleeves to indicate their class or level.

Children entered houses of refuge at the lowest rank and moved up by displaying good behavior. Bad behavior caused inmates to move down. Children at the top levels earned advantages like more free time, while those at the bottom might be sent to bed without supper. At the house of refuge in Providence, Rhode Island, inmates holding the lowest rank were "excluded almost entirely from the [other children]; not being permitted to join them in sports, or hold any conversation with them."

Inmates entering the Ohio Industrial School for Boys received a number of demerits that varied according to the seriousness of their crimes. Hard work and obedience erased the demerits, and when his slate was clean, a boy was free to leave.

Houses of refuge did allow the parents of inmates to visit their children, but not very often. Because the inmates had begun to develop the base habits attributed to the poor, superintendents wanted to keep them apart from their parents—the source of those habits—as much as possible. At the houses of refuge in New York and Philadelphia, parents could visit only once every three months. In Philadelphia, parents had to ask permission before speaking to their sons and daughters.

The boys and girls confined to houses of refuge aroused the sympathy of some Americans. Elijah Devoe observed a lonely little boy at the New York House of Refuge who befriended insects. He "would go about the yard with dozens of live beetles, and other bugs, thrust inside his shirt-bosom next to his skin," Devoe wrote. Another observer, a resident of Philadelphia, recalled seeing "little prisoners" thrusting their fists through the bars enclosing his city's institution, trying to sell flowers they had picked on the grounds. "The great throng of passers-by would stop and watch these little ones, and sometimes give a few cents for the flowers," he noted. "It was a sad sight—free children on the one side and the impris-oned ones, of the same age, in their coarse clothing, on the other."

Houses of refuge were far from a perfect solution to the problem of youthful crime. They admitted lawbreakers as young as seven and as old as twenty-one. This meant that small children were still being locked up with young adults who had repeatedly broken the law—with "large notorious & hardened villains," said Joseph Curtis of the New York House of Refuge. "I fear that . . . introducing these ill bred and hardened boys among the first and young offenders will prove a curse rather than a bless-ing." The Reverend John Stanford agreed with Curtis, commenting that children were graduating from houses of refuge with the "degree of Bachelor of Arts in crime."

Because of these and similar concerns, a different kind of institution emerged after 1850. The reform school, or reformatory, was strictly for first-time offenders. Most reformatories housed only boys, but some had quarters for girls as well. The first reform school just for girls opened in Massachusetts in 1854.

Teenage girls often were confined to reform schools not because they had committed crimes, but because they were sexually active. Case 888 from the records of the Massachusetts institution describes a girl who "has absented herself from home late evenings, and recently was away three days. She seeks the company of boys. . . ." Case 892 "made the acquain-tance of a bad girl in the neighborhood while her mother was at work, who led her astray." Parents also brought their daughters to reformatories because the girls had become too "stubborn" to manage at home.

To promote the idea that the staff and inmates of the Massachusetts Industrial School for Girls were one big family, the managers housed the girls in several buildings called cottages. Each cottage had its own matron, who acted as "mother" to as many as thirty girls, age seven through fif-teen. The older girls were to serve as big sisters to the younger ones in their cottage, offering guidance. Each cottage had a homey kitchen and

EXPOSTULATING WITH A VICIOUS GIRL.

A GRADUATE.

LEARNING TO COOK.

MAKING PAPER BOXES.

CONNECTICUT.—THE STATE INDUSTRIAL SCHOOL FOR GIRLS, AT MIDDLETOWN.—FROM SKETCHES BY A STAFF ARTIST.—SEE PAGE 198.

Scenes from the Connecticut Industrial School for Girls (*clockwise, from top*): The matron tries to reason with a new arrival, a "vicious girl"; inmates learn employable skills, such as making boxes; the girls receive instruction in domestic arts; a neatly dressed, fully reformed graduate displays her good manners.

living room—as well as a basement room for solitary confinement. And the girls slept in prisonlike cells.

More than a few young people died in houses of refuge and reform schools, and some escaped. Most remained behind the thick walls and served sentences of eighteen months to two years. Usually, at the end of that period, the authorities pronounced them rehabilitated and arranged for them to be apprenticed or indentured. Many of the boys who left the New York House of Refuge were apprenticed on farms, far from harmful city influences. Some went to sea on merchant or whaling ships for two years or longer. The first boy to leave the Philadelphia House of Refuge as an apprentice, Henry Saul, was bound to a Mr. Horace Cady of Lima, Peru, on June 24, 1829. Like female orphans, girls leaving houses of refuge and reformatories often became maidservants.

It was the policy of the Philadelphia House of Refuge that no child be apprenticed to a tavern keeper or distiller of whiskey. Girls were not to be placed with unmarried men. Each inmate leaving that institution received a Bible and a list of instructions on how to behave. But whether a child went to live with a kind or cruel master was determined by the luck of the draw. A small boy named John Jackson was separated permanently from his widowed mother when he was sent to the Philadelphia House of Refuge in the early 1850s. Within a few years he was bound to a Delaware farmer who starved and beat him. Four times he tried to escape and was recaptured; the fifth time he succeeded and went to sea.

Policies varied from one institution to another. Girls remained at the Massachusetts Industrial School for Girls until they turned sixteen, no matter how old they were when they entered the reformatory. They then spent two years as indentured servants under state supervision. Youths leaving the Ohio Industrial School for Boys received ten dollars and a new suit but were given no help finding a place to live or work. A missionary who labored on behalf of this school for more than thirty years estimated that three-fourths of the boys became productive citizens. A few returned to

The emblem of the Philadelphia House of Refuge. According to the scene depicted, boys entered the institution as budding criminals and departed as young gentlemen.

crime, "and of others," he remarked, "we may say, as of many a gallant vessel, she left port and was never heard from."

Managers publicized success stories and downplayed failures. A surprising number of apprentices—as many as four in ten—came back to houses of refuge because their masters had dismissed them for bad behavior or laziness. A few girls were dismissed in disgrace after being sexually abused. The victim commonly was blamed in the nineteenth century when sexual abuse of a female servant came to light.

Some young apprentices returned to their homes and families. Houses of refuge often declined, however, to tell parents where their children had been sent. The managers of the New York House of Refuge noted in April 1847: "We have parted with a large number of children this spring, and many [parents] who came expecting to find children here, went away disappointed."

 An urban American street child. Some people worried that, if left alone, the large population of children living on city streets might grow up into a dangerous political force.

CHAPTER 4

LET SOCIETY BEWARE!

His father and mother are wicked and bad,
And though their own child, they care not for the lad;
They give him no clothes, and no victuals to eat,
But send him to strangers, to beg of them meat.

—Miss Horwood, *The Deserted Boy*, 1817

Not everyone liked the idea of locking away poor and orphaned children. By the middle of the nineteenth century, critics were starting to complain that asylums, with their rigid schedules and strict rules, were more like factories than homes. They claimed that asylum managers failed to give inmates the love and individual attention that all children need. The real purpose of an asylum, they said, was to keep poor children out of sight.

Even people who favored institutional care had to admit that asylums could not house all the children needing help. Many were filled to capacity, yet cities still teemed with the outcast children of the poor. According to a report issued in 1849 by the New York City chief of police, about three thousand abandoned, orphaned, and runaway children were living on the streets of Manhattan. Other estimates for New York City were higher, ranging from ten thousand to thirty thousand. Some of the street children were orphans, but many had run away from home to escape alcoholic or violent parents. Others had been left behind by parents migrating west. There were even a number of children who had simply wandered off and become lost.

In the slums of New York and other cities, children picked through piles of garbage to find anything they might sell for a few pennies. Ragged boys begged from passersby, joined street gangs, and picked pockets, while barefoot girls as young as fourteen worked as prostitutes. Hungry, home-less, exhausted youngsters slept in alleys and entranceways.

It is hard for Americans of the twenty-first century to imagine how wretched these children were. A description of a seven-year-old beggar written by a New Yorker in 1858 provides some insight:

> *She was clothed in a filthy, tattered gown; her light brown locks were tangled and matted, and her little bare feet looked as blue as the cold pavement on which they rested. . . . Her face exhibited no light shades, save two or three white lines which vertically crossed one cheek, marking the course in which tears had flowed from the fountain of one large, dark eye, for the other was bandaged with a dirty rag.*

The loudest critic of asylums was Charles Loring Brace, a Connecticut-born minister who was to strongly influence how future generations cared for society's dependent children. "My observation has been, that where you have large numbers of children together, you cannot have that direct sympathy and interest and personal management which make the family so beneficial to children," Brace said. He insisted that asylums left young people unprepared for life, and he objected to their cost. He said, "The asylum system is, of necessity, immensely expensive, and can reach but a comparatively small number of subjects."

The orphanage was the wrong solution to the problem of street waifs, according to Brace. But so was doing nothing. Brace was convinced that, left alone today, these children would grow into the thieves and rioters of tomorrow. They might even join together and form a dangerous political force. "Let society beware," he warned, "when the outcast, vicious, reckless multitude of New York boys, swarming now in every foul alley and low street, come to know their power and use it!" The future of American cities was at stake.

Early in his career Brace had made up his mind not to preach from a church pulpit like most clergymen. He chose instead to work as a "city missionary," aiding the poor and homeless. In 1851, at age twenty-five, he settled in New York City and began doing the Lord's work at the Five Points Mission. Founded in 1848 by the Ladies' Methodist Home Missionary Society, the mission provided the people of Five Points with food, clothing, education, and, of course, the comforts of religion. Missionaries counseled the poor on the streets, in saloons, and at home.

Charles Loring Brace as a young man.

To reach the dwellings of the poor, Brace climbed dark staircases littered with trash and reeking of human waste. Once admitted, he saw ten or more people living in one room and children wrapped in rags to stay warm. Brace saw families so desperate that even with well-meaning parents, children had little hope for the future. After visiting one poverty-stricken woman and her family, Brace wrote, "Her husband had fever and

A homeless boy and his mother spend the night on snow-covered steps in this illustration from a Children's Aid Society publication.

ague [chills], and had fallen out of work; she had just borne her baby and could not do anything. *They did not know what to do.* Rent to pay, themselves to feed, fuel and all— and *no work!*"

Brace was struck by "the immense number of boys and girls floating and drifting about our streets with hardly any assignable home or occupation, who continually swelled the multitude of criminals, prostitutes, and vagrants." He led "Boys' Meetings" for the Five Points Mission, but these Sunday services for street youth were a terrible failure. Often, instead of sitting still and listening, the boys who had been rounded up threw rocks at the preachers, fought, and made noise.

In 1853, seeking a better way to help urban youth, several ministers formed the Children's Aid Society, with Brace as its first chief officer. Though he planned to spend only a year in the position, he ended up holding it for nearly forty. The main task of the Children's Aid Society was to place urban street orphans with families in the country, far from the city and its corruption. Brace believed that children belonged in secure, loving homes where they had enough to eat, slept in warm beds, and wore clean clothes. To him no child was past hope. "The habits and passions of the street boy or girl, can never be beyond the reach of kindly or religious influences," he said, adding that the children's "faults are to be mildly judged, in memory of the pressing temptations and the hard circumstances which have surrounded them." A strong, stable family, he said, was "God's reformatory."

At the start the Children's Aid Society found homes for children in New York State and New England. The first child to be "placed out" was thirteen-year-old John Quig, the son of a poor widow. The Children's Aid Society sent him to live with a family in rural East Woodstock, Connecticut, in April 1853.

In autumn 1854 the society rounded up forty-six children from the streets of Manhattan, most of them between the ages of seven and fifteen, and sent them to the Midwest. The Reverend E. P. Smith of the society escorted the orphans by boat and train to Dowagiac, Michigan. There, following a church service, Smith invited the local farmers and townspeople to choose among the "little ones of Christ," to select a boy or girl to take in and raise as their own. The children stood, patiently but warily, as strangers looked them over to decide if they appeared strong enough to work or charming enough to win a parent's love.

Orphans pose for a photograph in Kansas with the train that is transporting them to new homes in the Midwest.

People willing to be foster parents underwent no screening. No one investigated whether they were fit to raise a child. What's more, the adults who took children signed no articles of indenture. They consented verbally to provide food, clothing, and education for the orphans, just as they would for their own sons and daughters. In return for the chance to grow up in a family, a boy was expected to plow fields and harvest crops; a girl was expected to do housework and farm chores and watch younger children.

At the time, children commonly worked on farms in exchange for room and board. According to U.S. Census Bureau figures, between 1850 and 1900 one-fifth to one-third of farm homes contained children who were not the offspring of adults living in the household. Usually, though, these young people were the children of relatives or neighbors. Selecting a child from a group of strangers was something new.

The Children's Aid Society sent two more trainloads of children to the Midwest in January 1855, and many more in the months and years that followed. By 1860 the agency had placed more than five thousand children in foster homes; by 1884 Brace and his agents claimed to have relocated more than sixty thousand children throughout the United States. No one knows the exact number of children placed out, because the Children's Aid Society kept sloppy records. For the same reason, how most of the children got along in their new homes is also unknown.

Groups similar to New York's Children's Aid Society found rural homes for poor children from other cities. They included the Henry Watson Children's Aid Society of Baltimore and the Children's Aid Society of Pennsylvania. In 1865 a Michigan man wrote to the managers of a Boston group, the New England Home for Little Wanderers, "My friends want children between the ages of ten and fourteen, smart, active, and intelligent. I think that I could dispose of a whole carload of boys and girls if you could send them to me soon." Agencies had a tougher time placing children younger than ten, who were less able to do a productive day's work.

A group of boys about to travel west with the Children's Aid Society, thanks to a gift of money from Mrs. John Jacob Astor. The Astor family had amassed a fortune in the fur trade.

Also, nearly all the children placed were white. Agency managers knew that most white families would be unwilling to accept black children. But they made no effort to find black families wanting to take in poor boys and girls.

The trains that carried children west came to be known as orphan trains, but less than half of the young people relocated by the Children's Aid Society were full orphans. Only sixteen percent of the children placed in foster homes in 1854 and 1855 were truly alone, without home or family. Most of the others had been living at home with one or both parents. In nearly one-fourth of the cases, a parent had given up his or her child out of necessity. The records of the Children's Aid Society reveal that one thirteen-year-old boy was surrendered by a mother "too poor to support him." Another boy of the same age was the "son of a poor man—can't take care of him." The father who gave up a third child was a "broken down laborer."

In their eagerness to fill trains and clean the city's streets, Brace's agents collected youngsters carelessly. A child who claimed to be homeless was taken at his or her word. The Reverend Smith snatched one boy from the street hours before the first orphan train left for Dowagiac and picked up another child while changing trains in Albany, New York. In 1873 the society found homes for about three thousand children; the agents placed four hundred of those children in new homes without trying to find out whether their parents were living or dead.

The agents of the Children's Aid Society also assumed that most of the orphan-train riders lived happily ever after in their new homes. In 1900 Charles Loring Brace would boast of an eighty-seven percent success rate. Yet the society rarely checked on the children to see how they were faring. Its annual reports, written for people who contributed money to the society, contained letters from grateful youngsters, such as sixteen-year-old George, who had settled on a farm in Wayne County, New York, in 1855. George wrote, "I think that I like the country better than the city, for here

I can run and make as much noise as I please without disturbing the neighbors. . . . I thank you for putting me in such a nice home; I get along very well, and please them all."

"I am getting along first rate," wrote twelve-year-old Edward from his new home, a farm in Illinois. Edward had lost his parents to cholera. "I like to live here," his letter continued. "I believe I have got a good home; they are as good to me, as anybody would be. I went to school this summer, and I expect to go this winter. I have been well since I came here. I have been husking corn, and can beat any body of my size and age I believe."

Certainly, there were happy outcomes, but there were also instances of children being whipped, sexually abused, neglected, overworked, or underfed. Some foster parents threw up their hands when faced with a feisty, defiant street child. "She is a

The Children's Aid Society presented an ideal image of needy city children transplanted to the country. This picture from one of the society's publications shows a happy, thriving street boy after one year of farm life.

very bad girl," wrote the Illinois foster parent of a child named Elizabeth. "She is bad in the sense of impudent, stubborn, disobedient, hot tempered, and ungrateful; and on this account, she has made us all lead an unhappy life."

Because no legal contract bound them to their foster families, the children were free to leave at any time, and many of them did. Some ran away or went to live in other households, but often biological parents reclaimed their sons and daughters when things at home had improved. Even John Quig, the first child placed out by the Children's Aid Society, returned to New York City in December 1855, when his brother went to Connecticut to retrieve him.

The practice of placing children out had its critics, just as asylum care did. Roman Catholics cried out against the placement of Catholic children in Protestant households, which was common. Also, as time passed, many people in the Midwest grew to resent the influx of poor children from Eastern cities. It seemed that Easterners were dumping their problems on the Midwesterners' doorstep. In truth, the orphan-train children had proved themselves no more likely to break the law than children born and raised on farms; still, a number of states passed laws controlling the placement of children from out of state. Michigan enacted the first of these laws in 1887; by 1924 twenty-eight states from New Jersey to South Dakota had laws regulating child placement.

These laws called for foster homes to be investigated beforehand. They also required placing agencies to follow up on children in their new homes and to report on the children's welfare to the state or county. An agency placing a child within the state had to post a performance bond—that is, the agency had to put up money as a guarantee that it would perform its duties correctly. The laws barred the placement of children likely to become a public burden, such as those who were sick or disabled or who had a "vicious character."

The Children's Aid Society also helped children who remained in New York City by operating industrial schools and lodging houses. The agency ran schools specifically for children who held factory jobs during the day, offering nighttime instruction in reading, writing, and arithmetic and some job training. The volunteer teachers were mainly well-to-do women who paid particular attention to the girls, hoping to prevent them from becoming prostitutes. Girls attending the industrial schools learned hat making and dressmaking, while boys received training in carpentry, shoemaking, and other crafts.

The first such school, the Fourth Ward Industrial School, opened in a church basement shortly after the Children's Aid Society was founded. The Fourth Ward was a poor neighborhood in lower Manhattan. It was not the poorest in the city, but it was a depressing place nonetheless. Its

Children salute the American flag at the Mott Street Industrial School. Mott Street is located in a part of lower Manhattan where Italian immigrants began to settle in the 1850s. By 1880 Mott Street was largely Italian. Neighborhoods change, though, and today many Chinese immigrants live on or near Mott Street.

residents lived in crowded tenements that were dark and poorly ventilated. Fumes from the coal that was burned for fuel day after day irritated the noses and throats of Fourth Ward children. Less than half the homes were connected to sewers, so people disposed of wastes wherever they could— down sinks that led to outdoor cesspools, on streets and sidewalks, in gutters and backyards. Families often had to balance on planks to cross puddles of refuse in order to reach their homes. According to the federal census of 1860, most adults living in the Fourth Ward were seamen, laborers, unemployed persons, prostitutes, or "doubtful characters."

The Fourth Ward Industrial School was such a success that the society soon opened more schools throughout the city. Some offered lessons taught in German or Italian for the immigrant children living nearby. Some were exclusively for Jewish or African-American children. By 1901 the Children's Aid Society had founded at least twenty-five industrial schools in New York City.

The society also established lodging houses for the city's working children. The best-known of these was the Newsboys' Lodging House, which opened in March 1854. Boys hawking newspapers seemed to be everywhere in American cities in the nineteenth century. Their cries could be heard on the streets from morning until night. Many of these boys lived on their own and paid for food and a night's shelter from their meager earnings.

The original Newsboys' Lodging House, located in a loft above the offices of the *New York Sun,* a daily paper, contained forty beds. Six cents bought a boy a clean bed for the night and a bath in the large washroom. If he required a haircut, treatment for lice, or a new item of clothing or shoes, those needs were met as well. For another four cents a boy could have a meal in a dining hall that doubled as a schoolroom for night classes. He was welcome to enjoy books, periodicals, and the Bible in the reading room. Also, he was encouraged to put away a fraction of his earnings in the lodging house's Six-Penny Savings Bank.

Left: Newsboys seemed to be everywhere in American cities in the 1800s. Here an enterprising youth sells a paper to a merchant on a city dock.

Below: This illustration from a nineteenth-century periodical presents scenes from daily life at the Newsboys' Lodging House.

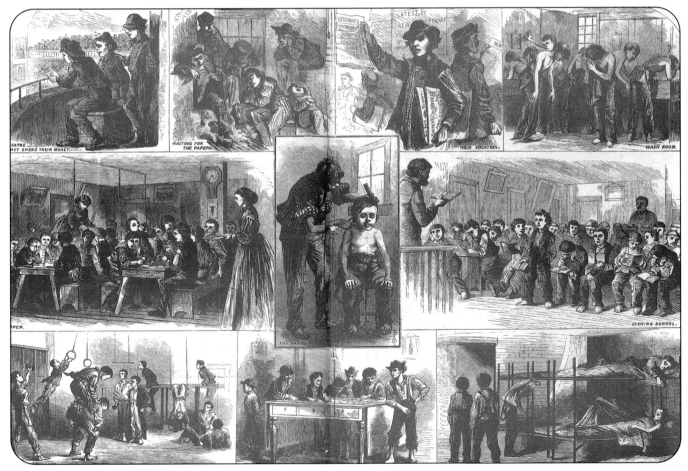

Boys at the Newsboys' Lodging House roll up dirty sleeves to wash their faces and hands, and then dry off on soiled towels.

At first, newsboys listened warily to lodging-house managers and suspected they were being tricked into attending Sunday school. But they soon recognized a good deal. The Newsboys' Lodging House did offer church services and talks on religion, but it was cheap and clean. A bed in one of the city's dirtiest flophouses cost more—seven cents a night.

About 400 boys slept in the Newsboys' Lodging House during its first year of operation. Boys came and went, staying an average sixteen nights throughout the year. In 1858 the Children's Aid Society opened a new and bigger Newsboys' Lodging House, this one furnished with 250 beds. Some 3,000 boys spent an average five nights in the new shelter during its first year of operation.

To Charles Loring Brace the newsboys' willingness to work hard and earn their way in the world ensured that they would be a credit to society. Rather than offer charity, he wanted to "treat the lads as independent little dealers," he said, to "give them nothing without payment."

 Sons of fallen Union fighting men,
residents of the Soldiers' Orphans' School
at Jumonville, Pennsylvania.

SOLDIERS' ORPHANS

"My father fell on the field of blood,—
And my mother in new-made grave doth lie;
Unbar the door, for the love of God—
The winter is cold," they cry.

—John A. Porter, "The House of Mercy," 1864

The number of boys seeking shelter at the Newsboys' Lodging House doubled once the Civil War began. Among the boys buying a bed and hot meal were sons of men who had died in uniform.

Roughly 620,000 men died in the Civil War, and many of them were husbands and fathers. (The exact number of children left fatherless by the war is unknown, but in the four years of fighting—from April 1861 through April 1865—thousands more orphans and half orphans suddenly needed care.) While some of the dead soldiers had been poor, most had earned a decent living as farmers, clerks, teachers, blacksmiths, carpenters, and the like. A man's death often meant the loss of a household's income and a family plunged into poverty. Widows tried to scrape by, but many found it beyond their ability to run a farm, make mortgage payments, and feed and clothe their young ones.

In July 1862 the federal government awarded pensions to the widows of soldiers and sailors who died in the war. The amount a woman received depended on her husband's military rank. Widows of the highest-ranking officers received thirty dollars a month, while the widows of privates and common sailors received only eight dollars a month. In 1866 Congress granted widows an extra two dollars per month for every child younger than sixteen. Then, in 1868, Civil War orphans under sixteen began to get a two-dollar pension of their own. The orphans received each month the same amount that a bricklayer's helper earned in a day, so even with these increases, the payments amounted to very little. Many young people who lost their fathers in the war remained in need.

Existing orphanages did what they could. In Philadelphia, for example, half the 160 youngsters housed in the Northern Home for Friendless Children during the war were soldiers' orphans. Daughters and sons of Union men filled asylums in Milwaukee, Boston, Louisville, and other cities both during and after the war. Protestant, Catholic, and Jewish groups responded to the need by establishing asylums for war orphans, and before long there was at least one home built expressly for soldiers' orphans in nearly every state.

Americans opened their hearts to the orphans of the Civil War as they never had done for the children of the urban poor. These were not the "vicious" children who preyed on honest working people, but the sons and daughters of men who had given their lives for freedom. Public sentiment was strongest after the Battle of Gettysburg, which was fought during the first three days of July 1863. This major battle left six to eight thousand bodies scattered across the fields and orchards of Gettysburg, Pennsylvania. As the townspeople undertook the grisly task of burying the Union and Confederate dead, they searched the corpses for clues to the men's identities.

Civil War soldiers worried about dying unknown. Some hung hand-made identity tags around their necks, pinned papers bearing their names

A likeness of the Humiston children adorned a piece of sheet music. James G. Clark's song "The Children of the Battle Field" was inspired by the story of Amos Humiston's death and the search for his identity.

to their clothing, or marked their names on belongings. Yet forty-two percent of the Civil War dead were never identified. (It was not until 1913 that the army made identity tags mandatory.)

One dead Union sergeant presented a sad puzzle. A burial crew had found his body in the secluded spot where he had crawled off to die. Nothing on the man revealed his name or military unit; a photograph of three children clutched in his fist was the only clue to who he was. It appeared he had been thinking of these dear ones at his moment of death. Dr. John Francis Bourns, who had gone to Gettysburg to treat wounded soldiers, was so intrigued with the mystery soldier that he took the photograph home to Philadelphia, vowing to identify the man.

On October 19, 1863, thanks to Bourns's efforts, *The Philadelphia Inquirer* printed a story titled "Whose Father Was He?" In it, the reporter imagined the soldier's final moments, using the sentimental writing style that nineteenth-century Americans seemed to love: "He has finished his work on earth . . . he has freely given his life to his country; and now, while his life's blood is ebbing, he clasps in his hands the image of his children, and, commending them to the God of the fatherless, rests his last lingering look upon them."

Newspapers in 1863 lacked the technology to publish photographs, so the writer described the children in the picture. He said that the oldest child, a boy, wore a shirt made from the same fabric as the dress on the middle child, a girl. The youngest boy wore a dark suit and sat on a chair between the others. The children looked to be nine, seven, and five years of age. Imagining the photograph being one day returned to the dead hero's family, the author wrote, "Of what inestimable value will it be to these children, proving, as it does, that the last thought of their dying father was for them, and them only."

As other newspapers reprinted the story and people throughout the country wondered about the battlefield orphans, one reader had a pretty good idea who they were. Mrs. Philinda Humiston of Portville, New York, read the account in November 1863 in the *American Presbyterian,* a church publication. She strongly suspected that the dead man was her husband and that the picture was of their children, Frank, Alice, and Fred, ages eight, six, and four. Several months earlier, Mrs. Humiston had mailed her husband a photograph of the children that seemed to match the one sketched in words. Even more worrisome, she had heard nothing from him since the Battle of Gettysburg. Mrs. Humiston wrote to Dr. Bourns, who sent her a copy of the photograph. Upon receiving it, she confirmed the identities of the children and of the dead soldier. He was indeed her husband, Sergeant Amos Humiston of the 154th New York Volunteer Infantry. Amos Humiston had been a harness maker before joining the Union army.

Now the press described Dr. Bourns's journey to Portville to return the original photograph and the widow's efforts to support her family as a seamstress. When newspapers spread the word about Dr. Bourns's next project, to build a home for Civil War orphans in Gettysburg, Americans from all walks of life contributed to the cause. Money came from Jay

The National Homestead at Gettysburg. The three Humiston children remained at the Homestead for three years, until their mother remarried. The entire family then moved to Massachusetts.

Gould, a ruthless businessman who was on his way to making a fortune in the stock market and in railroads, as well as from Sunday-school students who had saved their pennies. Bourns's organization, the National Orphans' Homestead Association, used the funds to buy a brick building on Gettysburg's Cemetery Hill. The orphanage, known as the National Homestead, opened in October 1866. Its most celebrated residents were the three Humiston children, whose mother had been hired to help run the home.

Some states opened asylums for their own war orphans. In 1870 Governor Rutherford B. Hayes of Ohio was stunned to learn that three hundred soldiers' orphans in his state were sleeping in poorhouses because they had nowhere else to go. As many as two thousand more Ohio children orphaned by the war had no homes at all. Hayes persuaded the legislature to pass a law establishing asylums for these children. Eight other states—New Jersey, Pennsylvania, Illinois, Indiana, Iowa, Kansas, Wisconsin, and Minnesota—also founded state-run soldiers' orphans' homes.

Concern for children orphaned by this terrible war had reached all the way to the White House. On March 4, 1865, in his Second Inaugural Address, President Abraham Lincoln asked the American people to "bind up the nation's wounds, to care for him who shall have borne the battle and for his widow and his orphan. . . ." The war was drawing to a close as Lincoln began his second term. To the president, caring for the orphans was part of the healing that had to begin.

Lincoln was assassinated on April 14, 1865, five days after the Civil War ended. Responsibility for the people's well-being fell to the next president, Andrew Johnson. In June 1866 Johnson called on Congress and the public to "take up the destitute orphans and educate and guide them," thereby laying "a solid moral basis which may control them throughout their future lives." Soon afterward, on July 25, 1866, Congress passed an act creating the National Soldiers' and Sailors' Orphan Home in Washington,

UNCLE SAM. "Go ahead, Boys: I'll take care of the Wives and Babies. GOD bless you!

Uncle Sam promises to care for the wives and children of men in uniform in this political cartoon from 1862.

D.C. Among its twenty-six women managers was a future first lady, Julia B. Grant.

By 1866 Pennsylvania had established thirty-six asylums, schools, and homes for 2,686 soldiers' orphans. The state's leaders hoped to mold the orphans into "respected men and fathers and honored women and mothers." The children spent long days in the classroom, from eight A.M. until four forty-five P.M. They all learned reading, writing, spelling, and arithmetic; students in the upper grades also had lessons in botany, philosophy, geography, algebra, and history. Saturday was a workday, when the girls spent the morning cleaning and the boys did farm chores. In the afternoon the girls exercised for an hour while the boys practiced military drills.

Children in the Pennsylvania homes received three outfits of clothing: one for school, one for work, and one for Sundays. It was the children's duty to keep their clothes clean and tidy. They had to pass an inspection every morning before breakfast. Anyone whose face, hands, or ears showed signs of dirt, or whose clothing was torn or missing a button, had to correct the flaw before sitting down to eat. Once a week the staff conducted a more rigid inspection to look for skin diseases and parasites.

Thomas Henry Burrowes, superintendent of the homes, insisted on good manners at the table. He was less harsh than earlier asylum managers

Left: Suetta Markley, a resident of a Pennsylvania soldiers' orphans' home, in the clothing typical of girls in these state-run asylums. *Right:* Inmate John Wilhelm in the uniform worn by boys in Pennsylvania's soldiers' orphans' homes.

SUETTA MARKLEY.

JOHN WILHELM.

about talking during meals, asking only that a "reasonable degree of silence shall be maintained while eating." Burrowes had been a member of the state legislature, a farmer, and state superintendent of schools before overseeing the orphans' homes. He believed in the benefits of "wholesome, sufficient, and regular food," and insisted that only healthy meals be served. Breakfast was to include bread with butter or molasses; coffee, tea, hot chocolate, or sweetened milk; and one or more of the following: fried or boiled potatoes, fried or boiled eggs, fish, hash, and other meat dishes. Dinner was bread and meat served with one or more cooked vegetables and possibly soup, salad, or applesauce. Supper was bread with butter or molasses; coffee, tea, or milk; and one or more of these foods: cold meat, stewed fruit, potatoes, onions, corn bread, and soup. The children had fruit at any meal when it was in season and cake or pie on Sundays.

To help the children of its fallen heroes, the state of Wisconsin took over a private soldiers' orphan asylum in March 1866. This orphanage was in the city of Madison, in a three-story, eight-sided structure that had been a private home. Eighty-five children lived there in early 1866; by 1868 about three hundred lived there. Space was so tight that the staff set up racks to dry clothes in the kitchen and dining room.

Despite the crowding, the Wisconsin soldiers' orphan home provided a better education than most of the state's public schools. The children had lessons in arithmetic, geography, grammar, reading, music, health, and manners. With so many pupils to manage, the four teachers put up with no nonsense. A boy named Harry Dankoler, who entered the asylum in 1870, recalled being "several times punished for too much laughing in my classes." He said that the "laughing was thrashed out of me."

Punishments were severe at the Iowa Soldiers' Orphans Home at Cedar Falls when George Gallarno went to live there in October 1866. The superintendent "was a man of fiery red hair and also of fiery temper," Gallarno said. This combination, Gallarno believed, "accounted for his sternness in dealing with the children. . . . The children resented his treat-

The children and staff of the Wisconsin Soldiers' Orphans' Home, circa 1870.

ment and several of the more adventurous, to escape it, ran away from the Home." Most escapees came back to the asylum, having been recaptured by the superintendent or returned by their mothers. The trustees of the home received numerous complaints about this superintendent and replaced him with a kinder man in January 1867.

George Gallarno was typical of many soldiers' orphans. His father, an artilleryman, had died of typhoid on September 22, 1864, while encamped at Little Rock, Arkansas. George's mother had struggled for two years to feed and shelter her five children. "What battles my mother fought in caring for us, I never knew," Gallarno said. At last, his mother gave up and placed seven-year-old George and his brothers and sisters in the state's care.

The asylum at Cedar Falls, one of three state-run soldiers' orphans' homes in Iowa, was operating in a rundown hotel when the Gallarno children moved in. The old, rambling building always needed repairs, so in 1869 the state constructed a new asylum of bricks. The new orphanage sat in the center of a forty-acre tract that had been donated by the citizens of Cedar Falls.

On Saturdays the managers granted a half holiday to those boys who had behaved well during the week. "Those Saturday afternoon holidays—what memories they bring back!" a grown-up George Gallarno said. "How we trooped in freedom to the city at times, and in season to the fields and woods!" City outings often included a stop at Jorgensen's bakery for cake or candy. In the country the boys jumped into the swimming hole on a nearby farm. They climbed hills and snacked on wild plums and crabapples. (Girls remained in the asylum, no matter how good they had been. In the nineteenth century boys typically had more liberty than girls did.)

Boys march in military fashion outside the Soldiers' Orphan School at Phillipsburgh (now Phillipsburg), Pennsylvania.

While encamped at Washington, D.C., officers of Company F, 2nd Regiment, Rhode Island Volunteer Infantry, were photographed with several African Americans who had fled slavery, including a child.

"In the town of Cedar Falls, the citizens had no trouble separating the 'Home boys' from the 'town boys,'" Gallarno said. The boys from the orphans' home dressed alike in brown jeans. The girls wore cotton or wool dresses, and if they were twelve or older, they sewed their own clothes.

Americans built as many orphanages in the 1860s as they had in the twenty years leading up to the Civil War. Yet there were never enough asylums for all the children orphaned or made poor by the war. The children of dead Confederate fighting men had an especially tough time, because Southern communities could build only a handful of orphanages for them.

After losing the war, the South lacked the money and materials needed for new construction. Thousands of Confederate soldiers' orphans were forced to seek shelter wherever they could find it, frequently in poorhouses and reformatories.

The war left another group of children in need of care: the African-American boys and girls left homeless following the breakdown of slavery. When the Union army moved into the South, hundreds of thousands of African Americans sought the soldiers' protection. Most had escaped their owners' plantations, but some had been abandoned by white masters fleeing the Union invaders. The Northern soldiers called these African Americans "contrabands," using a term applied to enemy goods seized in war. The Confederates viewed their slaves as property, and apparently so did many of the troops fighting for the slaves' freedom.

The army put able-bodied African-American men to work building fortifications, roads, and bridges. Beginning in May 1862 the Union enlisted many of these men as soldiers. Some African-American boys also served the Union cause, as drummers and officers' servants. But the women and children among the contrabands often reached army camps exhausted and malnourished. The journey to freedom had left many of them ill, injured, or suffering from exposure to cold and rain.

Hungry, despairing women, children, and old men settled in muddy, makeshift camps alongside Union army posts throughout the South—on the banks of the Mississippi River and near Murfreesboro and Clarksville, Tennessee; Helena, Arkansas; and other towns. Some refugees lived in tents or packing crates, while others crowded into deserted houses, sheds, and stables. Children walked around in rags, without shoes or underwear, begging food from the soldiers, and babies went without diapers. People died every day from hunger and disease.

In time, a few private citizens opened asylums for the orphaned and abandoned children who were such a common sight in contraband camps. Lucy Gaylord Pomeroy, wife of Senator Samuel C. Pomeroy of Kansas, headed a group of Republican women who in 1863 founded one of these institutions, a home for African-American orphans and old women in Washington, D.C. After the war the Freedmen's Bureau, a government agency that helped former slaves adjust to life as free Americans, opened asylums for black children in New Orleans; Charleston, South Carolina; and other cities.

The asylums for African Americans were always overflowing with children and always short of supplies. There were never enough blankets or clothes to go around. In September 1863 a Northern missionary running an African-American asylum in Norfolk, Virginia, lamented that the boys in her care had "nothing but ragged pants to wear . . . we put patch upon patch but they are generally thin."

Meanwhile, in the North, soldiers' orphans became living symbols of

Soldiers' orphans place flags on their fathers' graves in Glenwood Cemetery, Philadelphia, on Memorial Day 1876.

patriotism. They were frequently called upon to take part in parades and civic ceremonies. Boys marched and performed military drills, and boys and girls decorated soldiers' graves. On May 30, 1868, children from the National Soldiers' and Sailors' Orphan Home helped to observe the first Memorial Day at the new national cemetery at Arlington, Virginia, across the Potomac River from Washington, D.C. Before the war the mansion and grounds at Arlington had been the home of Confederate General Robert E. Lee and his family. After the Lees abandoned the property, the Union army turned Arlington's rolling hills into a burial ground for men who had died in battles fought around the national capital. (Today the dead at Arlington represent every branch of the armed forces and every major U.S. military conflict. The remains of soldiers from the American Revolution, War of 1812, and Mexican War have even been reburied there.)

Arlington National Cemetery, Memorial Day 1929: Americans decorate the graves of soldiers killed in World War I. High government officials, military leaders, and veterans from all fifty states continue to be buried at Arlington, the nation's most important military cemetery.

As a crowd watched on that day in 1868, the children led a procession to the Tomb of the Unknown Dead of the Civil War, a vault holding the unidentified remains of 2,111 soldiers from nearby battlefields. The orphans sang a song; then, while the Fifth Cavalry Band played a somber march, they decorated the tomb with flags and flowers. Following a reading of Lincoln's Gettysburg Address, the orphans joined war veterans to place flowers and miniature flags on twelve thousand Union and Confederate graves throughout the cemetery.

Seven hundred miles away, in Madison, Wisconsin, on the same day, residents of the state's soldiers' orphans' home marched to the local cemetery. They carried flags and a banner that proclaimed them "The Adopted Children of Wisconsin." Following prayers and a song, they put flowers on soldiers' graves.

For a time the asylums for Civil War orphans filled a great need. Then the children who lived in them grew up and moved out. By 1900 most soldiers' orphans' homes had closed. Those still operating had become asylums for needy children of veterans of later wars. The Wisconsin Soldiers' Orphans' Home closed in 1874, after the board of trustees found homes for the last of the young people living there. In 1879 the National Soldiers' and Sailors' Orphan Home stopped admitting children and began preparing to close.

A scandal led to the closing of the National Homestead at Gettysburg.

The Indiana Soldiers' and Sailors' Orphans' Home Band performed for a convention of Union Civil War veterans at the start of the twentieth century. By this time all the children orphaned by the Civil War were grown. These boys were the sons of veterans of later conflicts.

In 1876 Matron Rosa Carmichael was convicted of assaulting a child. She continued to work at the home, but there were more allegations of abuse. It was even said that Carmichael chained children in a basement dungeon. In June 1877, after Dr. Bourns was accused of mismanaging the home's funds, the outraged editor of the *Gettysburg Star and Sentinel* stated: "The general conviction in this community is that the Homestead has outlived its usefulness and that the sooner it is closed the better." Authorities found homes for the nine children remaining in the institution, and it closed at the end of the year.

The soldiers' orphans' home at Cedar Falls, Iowa, closed in June 1876. Fifty years later George Gallarno wrote:

Sometimes the children at the Home felt they were abused; sometimes we complained of the food given us; sometimes we found fault with the clothing we were compelled to wear; and sometimes we grieved at the rules under which we lived. But today, as I look back through the years and recall the fact that our bodies were kept healthy through wholesome food and judicious exercise, and that our minds were turned to the right paths, I am more than ever convinced that Iowa . . . never put its heart and soul into a better or more benign work than that of looking after and caring for the orphans of its civil war soldiers.

 An image of ideal motherhood
from the Gilded Age.

EVERYBODY'S BUSINESS

Unknown, ideal, unseen mother,
Whom I love though I have known not,
Whom I worship unremembered. . . .

—LONNIE LOYLE, "A TRIBUTE," 1900

$\mathcal{I}$n the late nineteenth century, middle-class American women read books that taught them how to be model parents. According to one, *Woman's Work in the Home*, mothers had the power to "mould the entire future of mankind." They could accomplish this, the author said, "by doing their utmost to secure that the childhood of their boys and girls shall be as happy as outward circumstances render possible."

Americans' ideas about children were changing. Prosperous middle-class Americans had come to view childhood as a time of purity and innocence. They believed that children benefited from nurturing and protecting, from spending less time at work and more at play. Psychologists were teaching that children needed play for healthy development, so middle-class children spent their early years in toy-filled home nurseries. Many fathers commuted from newly built suburbs to city offices, leaving mothers to provide most of the children's care.

Life and the landscape were also changing. The United States had entered the Gilded Age, a period of great industrial growth that lasted from about 1875 through the early twentieth century. It was a time when greedy, driven men built great commercial empires at the expense of their competition. Business practices were poorly regulated, allowing corporate giants such as John D. Rockefeller and Andrew Carnegie to control the production of oil, steel, and other commodities. The typical American family—the one portrayed in magazines—lived in a city or suburb and was middle class. But the picture of wealth and comfort that the United States presented to the world was a thin coat of glittering paint that threatened to crack.

Beneath the sheen lay trouble. The U.S. population was exploding, as millions of immigrants arrived from southern and eastern Europe and from other parts of the world. Many of these new immigrants came from tiny villages. Unable to speak English and with few skills to offer city employers, they were forced to take menial jobs and live in dark, dirty tenement homes. These tenements were as dismal in the Gilded Age as they were when Charles Loring Brace visited the poor in the 1850s. Without trash collection, people tossed garbage out windows and down air shafts, or they left it on roofs to be carried away by the breeze. Several families would share a single privy that was located in a yard, cellar, or hallway and seldom cleaned. Tenants climbed shaky, broken staircases, and rats and roaches scurried everywhere. "The buildings are in such miserable repair . . . that if the wind could only reach them they would soon be toppling about the heads of their occupants," wrote an inspector from the New York Sanitary Aid Society in 1887. The Sanitary Aid Society was a charitable group concerned with public health.

Children in city slums had no space for play except trash-filled lots and busy streets, where they came in contact with criminals and prostitutes.

Jacob Riis, a writer and photographer who brought the living conditions of New York City's poor to the public's attention, described a boy growing up in an urban slum: "Home, the greatest factor of all in the training of the young, means nothing to him but a pigeonhole in a coop along with so many other human animals."

As the eastern seaboard teemed with people, Americans pushed west, causing cities like Chicago, Kansas City, Denver, and San Francisco to grow rapidly. Chicago, a lakeshore settlement of one hundred people in 1830, had a population of five hundred thousand in 1880. By 1890 its population had topped one million. With the influx of people came the same social problems that cities in the East faced: poverty, crime, and large numbers of poor and abandoned children. "How to care for the children

Italian immigrant children play on a New York City sidewalk in the early twentieth century.

of the very poor, and often depraved, part of the population of cities, is one of the most serious of public questions," said Josephine Shaw Lowell, the first woman commissioner of the New York State Board of Charities. Lowell's organization oversaw the work of public and private agencies serving the needy in her state.

Among the institutions visited by boards of charities in New York and other states were poorhouses. Although orphanages had been built partly to rescue children from such places, thousands of girls and boys continued to live in shelters for the poor. In 1868 the secretary of the Ohio Board of State Charities reported on the sad conditions in the poorhouses of his state. He described one ten-year-old inmate, unable to hear or speak, whose father had been killed in the Civil War. This boy lived alone, locked inside a cell. His nearest neighbor was an insane woman who tossed feces at him through broken panels in her cell door. "He was crying bitterly," the secretary wrote, "and, on being released, made signs indicating that he was very hungry." Other children in poorhouses suffered just as much.

Reports such as this one caught the attention of lawmakers. On April 24, 1875, New York became the first state to outlaw the placement of children in poorhouses. Ohio, Pennsylvania, Indiana, and other states soon passed similar laws. The legislation left it up to counties within a state to pay private asylums to care for children removed from poorhouses or to house them in county-run orphanages. The laws helped, but they were badly enforced, and many county officials moved slowly. As a result, nearly eight thousand American children between the ages of two and sixteen were still living in poorhouses in 1880.

The laws did nothing to help the disabled. The New York law made it a crime to keep any child between the ages of three and sixteen in a poorhouse "unless such child be an unteachable idiot, an epileptic or paralytic, or . . . otherwise defective, diseased or deformed. . . ." Asylums still took only healthy children who had no special needs, which meant that youngsters like the deaf boy in Ohio were often out of luck.

The Massachusetts Board of Lunacy and Charity took custody of these neglected children in the early 1890s. The board oversaw the care of prisoners, the poor, and the mentally ill.

Father Charles Neale Field, an Episcopal priest, opened St. Augustine Farm, an asylum for African-American children, in Foxboro, Massachusetts, in 1891.

Another group of overlooked children did receive aid: young people who endured physical abuse at home. Child abuse occurs at every economic level and in every ethnic and racial group. But the stresses of nineteenth-century tenement life—including poverty, unemployment, and alcoholism—caused many parents to lash out at their children. It was an everyday event for poor youngsters to be beaten, kicked, or even maimed at home, but one that caused little comment. "What is everybody's business is nobody's business" was the ironic comment of a Chicago charity worker. At the start of the Gilded Age many people were quick to say that some children were "vicious" and deserved harsh treatment. They believed that parents were within their rights to discipline their sons and daughters as they saw fit.

The mistreatment of one little girl and one woman's efforts to protect her led to changes that helped many. In 1873, while visiting an aged, dying woman, a New York City missionary named Etta Wheeler heard cries of pain coming from the tenement apartment next door. Neighbors told Wheeler that the cries came from a child who was being beaten, and they begged her to help. Wheeler knocked on the door of the apartment, the home of Francis and Mary Connolly, and forced her way inside. There she discovered ten-year-old Mary Ellen Wilson chained to a bedpost. The child was covered with bruises and cuts. Wheeler learned that Mary Ellen had been abandoned by her mother as an infant and knew no other family than the Connollys.

When a horrified Wheeler reported the couple to the police, she was outraged to learn that law enforcement could do nothing. In order for the police to step in, an eyewitness to the abuse would have to testify that the child's life was in danger. Charities also looked the other way. This was a family matter, they said.

There were laws to protect animals, though, so Wheeler told the story of Mary Ellen to Henry Bergh, president of the American Society for the Prevention of Cruelty to Animals (ASPCA). ASPCA agents were empowered to arrest anyone breaking the state's laws against cruelty to animals. After listening to Wheeler, Bergh and his lawyer, Elbridge Gerry, did something that had never before been done in a case like this: They persuaded a judge to issue a subpoena requiring the Connollys to appear in court. ASPCA agents removed Mary Ellen from the Connolly home, and the organization assumed custody of her, as it would do with a battered dog or horse.

On April 9, 1874, all parties appeared in court. Among the spectators was the writer Jacob Riis, who described the day's events. "I saw a child

Left: Mary Ellen Wilson exhibits her wounds in this photograph taken soon after her rescue by the ASPCA. *Right:* With time and proper care, Mary Ellen's cuts and bruises healed.

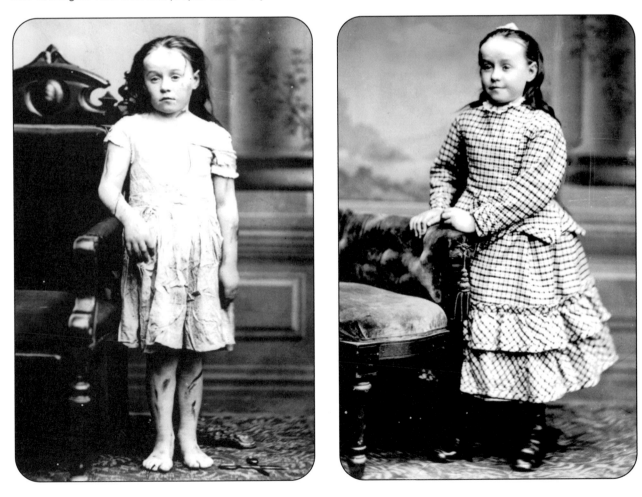

brought in, carried in a horse blanket, at the sight of which men wept aloud," Riis stated. "I saw it laid at the feet of the judge, who turned his face away. . . ." The crowd in the courtroom stared at the little girl's legs, which were covered with welts, and at a deep wound on her face, which she had received when Mrs. Connolly attacked her with scissors.

Henry Bergh addressed the court, saying, "The child is an animal. If there is no justice for it as a human being, it shall at least have the rights of the cur in the street. It shall not be abused."

Mary Ellen Wilson also spoke, referring to Mrs. Connolly as Mamma. The men and women present strained their ears to hear the child's halting voice. "I am never allowed to play with any children or to have any company whatever. Mamma has been in the habit of whipping and beating me almost every day," Mary Ellen said. "I have no recollection of ever having been kissed by any one. I have never been taken on Mamma's lap and caressed or petted. I never dared speak to anybody, because if I did I would get whipped. . . . Whenever Mamma went out, I was locked up in the bedroom." The judge had heard enough. He ordered Mary Ellen to be placed in an asylum. Mrs. Connolly was convicted of assault and sentenced to a year in jail.

Victory in the Connolly case inspired Bergh and Gerry to form the Society for the Prevention of Cruelty to Children (SPCC). On April 21, 1875, the New York state legislature granted the SPCC permission to work with the courts. The organization was to remove children from abusive homes and bring their parents to justice. The SPCC also lobbied for state laws to protect children, including an 1876 act that required parents and guardians to provide children with proper food, clothing, medical care, and supervision. This law made it a crime to harm or endanger a child. With the law backing it up, the SPCC sent nearly one hundred thousand abused and neglected children to orphanages between 1876 and 1903.

Reformers in other cities followed the example set by Bergh and Gerry.

In 1877 the Chicago Society for the Prevention of Cruelty to Animals changed its name to the Illinois Humane Society. It broadened its scope and worked to protect children as well as beasts. Agents of this society removed numerous children from abusive homes, including a twelve-year-old girl whose mother had poured a kettle of boiling water on her. They helped two children, ages seven and nine, whose father beat them daily with a broomstick. "[The father's] defense was that the children were liars," said Oscar L. Dudley, one of the society's founders, who later served in the state legislature. The Illinois Humane Society was too late to help eleven-year-old Max Gilman,

Henry Bergh served for life as a director of the SPCC, but his main concern remained the ASPCA and "the poor, dumb animals, which have not speech to tell how much they suffer."

whose stepfather beat him to death in 1888, but it worked for the killer's conviction and saw him sentenced to life in prison.

With children being removed from almshouses and abusive homes, it was plain to many people that the United States still needed asylums, perhaps more than ever. So even as homes for soldiers' orphans closed, Americans opened new institutions for poor and abandoned children. They founded more than four hundred orphanages between 1890 and 1903. Epidemics continued to add to the asylum population, and so did downturns in the economy, which put many parents out of work.

County and state governments established many of the new asylums. The largest of these was the Michigan State Public School, which opened in the town of Coldwater in 1874. Children entered this home only if

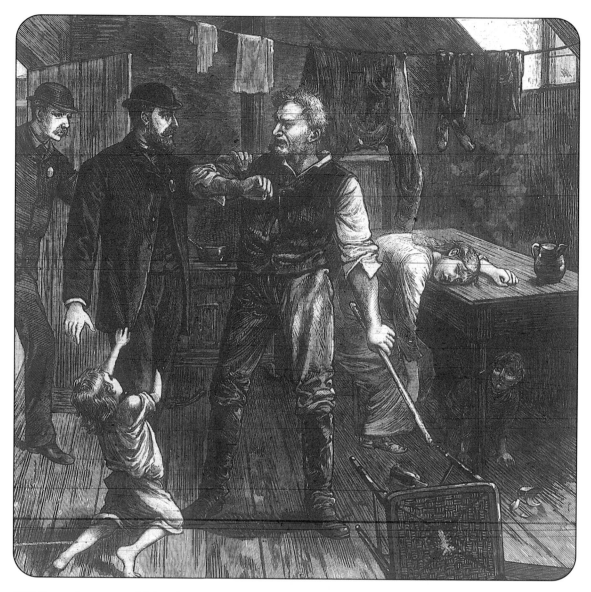

SPCC agents remove children from the care of an abusive father. The home appears to be the attic dwelling of a poor family. Note the broken whiskey bottle on the floor.

their parents or guardians surrendered all rights. They lived in the asylum a short time, just until the state placed them with a foster family.

More Jewish asylums appeared as immigration from eastern Europe increased. In 1880 eighty-five thousand Jews lived in the United States. Twenty years later the Jewish population was nearly half a million.

Supporting widows and orphans had been a Jewish tradition for centuries. Both the Old Testament and the Talmud (ancient writings on Jewish law) call on the faithful to aid these two groups.

Jewish charitable groups opened orphan asylums in Atlanta, New Orleans, Baltimore, Boston, Milwaukee, San Francisco, and other cities throughout the country. These asylums provided shelter, care, education, and instruction in the Jewish faith. Teaching the orphans to speak English and to understand American culture and values was another important task, since most were the children of immigrants. Young people often traveled long distances to reach these asylums: The Cleveland Jewish Orphan Asylum, which opened in 1868, accepted orphans and half orphans from fifteen states in the Midwest and South, and the Baltimore Hebrew Orphan Asylum welcomed children from Maryland, Georgia, South Carolina, Virginia, and Washington, D.C.

Catholic orphanages also grew in number. The laws that removed children from almshouses required them to be placed where they would receive instruction in their own religious faith. Public institutions claimed not to favor any one religion, but nineteenth-century America was largely Protestant. Many Catholics and Jews feared that children of their faiths were being taught Protestant beliefs in public asylums, so they opened institutions of their own.

Orphanages for African-American children continued to be founded as well. One of these was the Steele Home for Needy Children in Chattanooga, Tennessee. The Steele Home was established by a wealthy white woman, Almira S. Steele, in 1884, when black children were excluded from local asylums following a yellow-fever epidemic. Some local whites found the idea of a white woman caring for black children so horrifying that they burned the asylum to the ground just a few months after it opened. The staff and children escaped, and Almira Steele rebuilt the orphanage using a small insurance settlement and her own money.

The new middle-class attitudes toward children changed the care that

Left: Clara and Mary Radintz, ages three and four, on August 17, 1892, the day they entered the State Public School at Owatonna, Minnesota. The girls' mother was in a hospital for the mentally ill. Their father, said state officials, was "cruel and brutal."

Above: This drawing shows the Radintz sisters clean and neatly dressed—but not especially happy—as residents of the State Public School.

orphans received in asylums. Many orphanages now had larger washrooms and more bathtubs. Most orphans ate ample meals and a greater variety of foods, and the grounds of many asylums had playgrounds and ball fields.

Asylum children now left the institution to attend church and school. Managers encouraged mingling with the community to make the children's lives more like those of youngsters living with their families. Also, now that most towns had public schools, it cut costs to send the children out to school rather than hire teachers to conduct lessons in the asylum.

More than in the past, a matron acted as a "kind mother to all the little unfortunates under her control," as a writer for the New Haven, Connecticut, *Journal & Courier* noted in 1873. The matron at the New Haven Orphan Asylum began her motherly duties each day by visiting the dormitories and wishing the children a good morning. She presided over their daily prayers, and she supervised their personal care. Every morning the children's heads were scrubbed and combed to control lice. Every Saturday they had a bath and put on clean clothes. In summer their hands and feet were washed before bed. The matron spent her free time with the children, just as a middle-class mother would. She sewed their clothes, mended their stockings, and cut their hair.

Like middle-class youngsters who lived at home, asylum children received fewer beatings and harsh punishments in the late 1800s. Corporal punishment agitated the "excessively delicate organization of the brain," wrote the author of a popular child-rearing guide. "If the parent or teacher has tact or skill enough, and practical knowledge enough of the workings of the youthful mind," the author continued, "he can gain all the necessary ascendancy over it without resort to the violent infliction of bodily pain in any form."

Following the trend in society, asylum staff reasoned with rule breakers—at least as a first step. The directors of the Home for Destitute Children in Brooklyn, New York, reported in 1880 that "the matron appeals to their sense of right before she resorts to corporal punishment." At other institutions misbehaving youth were assigned extra chores, given less to eat, or placed in solitary confinement. At the New York Colored Orphan Asylum and other places, staff members rewarded good behavior in the hope of preventing bad. At another asylum, the Charleston Orphan House, children received demerits every time they violated a rule. These counted for more than black marks against a child's name. Anyone who piled up a hundred demerits "faced immediate indenture and the end of childhood."

New York's Hebrew Orphan Asylum held three fire drills a month at the start of the twentieth century. The girls could vacate the building in three minutes.

Unlike the administrators of the Michigan State Public School, some asylum managers now rejected the notion that severing family ties was in a child's best interest. A number of institutions let parents retain custody of their children, hoping to reunite families one day. These managers were learning from the new profession of social work, which took a scientific approach to helping people. Social workers studied the poor in their environment and looked at how the economy affected people's lives. They worked to improve living conditions and taught the poor to help themselves. They offered solutions based on observations rather than morals. Social work attracted recent college graduates, especially young women eager to pursue careers.

Pioneering social workers opened settlement houses, which were community centers in urban immigrant slums. The staff lived in a settlement house, becoming becoming neighbors to the people they served. Settlement houses offered job training, English classes, health care, and after-school recreation. Unlike poorhouses and asylums, which sheltered people in crisis, settlement houses reached out to self-supporting families as well, to prevent people from falling into poverty and to provide them with education and benefits that they could not obtain on their own.

In 1886 a student of philosophy named Stanton Coit founded the first settlement house in the United States, the Neighborhood Guild, on the Lower East Side of New York. Coit was a leader in the Ethical Culture Movement, which works to create a more humane society through education and community service. He believed that each person offered support by a settlement house would go on to help others. "The superior development of one member of a family or of a circle of friends may prove the social salvation of all the rest," he wrote. By 1900 a hundred settlement houses were serving the poor in U.S. cities. By 1918 the number would grow to four hundred.

Despite the teachings of social workers, life within asylum walls was still harsh. Illness remained a problem, with scarlet fever, whooping cough, measles, and other diseases continuing to claim orphans' lives. There were twelve deaths at one institution, the Chicago Nursery and Half-Orphan Asylum, in 1886, fourteen in 1890, and nineteen in 1892. Nearly all occurred among the youngest children.

Also, it came to light that some cruel and cunning adults had gone into the orphan-asylum business to live well on contributions meant for the children. In 1879 the SPCC exposed the shocking conditions at the Shepherd's Fold, a New York City orphanage run by a clergyman. This man and his wife lived comfortably, while the twenty-six children in their care were confined to a dank cellar and barely survived on watered-down milk, bread, and handfuls of beans. Every child among them was thin, pale, and ill.

Children play at Chicago's Hull House, possibly the most famous settlement house in the United States. Hull House was founded in 1899 by social reformers Jane Addams and Ellen Gates Starr.

The children, nuns, and priests of St. Mary's Orphanage, Galveston, Texas, were photographed in 1892. Eight years later, on September 8, 1900, a tremendous hurricane devastated Galveston and demolished the orphanage, killing ninety children and ten Sisters of Charity, including two pictured here. In all, more than six thousand people died in the great storm. The orphans at St. Mary's came from every part of Texas and ranged in age from two to fourteen. The names of the children in this photograph are unknown.

The Shepherd's Fold came to the attention of the SPCC when one starving five-year-old needed hospital care. The agency wasted no time bringing the villainous minister to trial. He was sentenced to a year in prison, and the Shepherd's Fold was shut down. The children returned to their families or went to live in other institutions.

In the final decades of the nineteenth century the United States stopped being a nation that left the care of dependent children up to families, churches, and charities. State and local governments stepped in, bringing abusive adults to justice and building asylums. These children became everyone's concern, but not everyone liked what was being done.

 The historic 1909 White House Conference on the Care of Dependent Children brought together leading child-care professionals and members of the clergy.

CHAPTER 7

THIS ARMY OF CHILDREN

Oh, when I am grown . . .
There'll be many to love me, and nothing to vex me,
No knots in my sewing, no crusts to my bread.
My days will go by like the days in a story,
The sweetest and gladdest that ever was read.

—MARGARET JOHNSON, "DAY DREAMS," CA. 1890

In 1909 President Theodore Roosevelt brought together child-care experts and religious leaders from throughout the United States to talk about needy children. "The interests of the nation are involved in the welfare of this army of children," the president said. For two days in January asylum managers, social workers, and representatives of charitable groups met at the White House with ministers, priests, and rabbis. The group emerged from the conference with a document outlining a national policy on the care of children.

The experts advised the nation to do everything in its power to keep children in their own homes. "Home life is the highest and finest product of civilization," they wrote. "Children should not be deprived of it except for urgent and compelling reasons." Poverty alone was not a compelling reason for removing children from their homes, they said. Parents in financial need deserved whatever aid was necessary to keep their families together. As a result of this directive, in 1910 New Jersey became the first state to provide monthly payments to widows and deserted wives. In New Jersey, and soon in other states as well, "mothers' aid" kept many children out of asylums and at home with their families.

The experts stated further, "Homeless and neglected children, if normal, should be cared for in families, when practicable." They said that foster care was the best choice for children unable to live with a parent or legal guardian. Orphanages were to be a last resort, and children's stays in them were to be brief.

At the time, about 110,000 children were living in institutions, and another 176,000 lived in foster homes. But thousands more needy youngsters were receiving no aid at all. According to one estimate, there were more than 120,000 homeless babies in the United States, in addition to tens of thousands of older children living on city streets.

In the early twentieth century legal adoption was becoming popular as a way for childless married couples to raise families. In fact, the Children's Aid Society had ended its "orphan train" program in the 1920s and was working instead to find parents to adopt children legally. Almost all adoptive parents were well-off whites who wanted babies or very young children of their own race. Massachusetts had passed the first law regulating adoption in 1851. By 1929 adoption laws were in effect in all forty-eight states. These laws protected the children's right to adoptive parents who were capable of bringing them up well. They required investigations of would-be parents, and in some cases called for follow-up home visits by trained personnel. The number of children legally adopted in the United States before the 1950s is unknown, but it is thought to have been smaller than the number in asylums or foster care.

Some orphanages responded to the demand by creating nurseries to house adoptable babies, but new, specialized agencies arranged most legal adoptions. These agencies often were founded by wealthy women to find homes for infants born to poorer single mothers. Americans of the early twentieth century generally viewed unmarried women and their babies as incomplete families, so despite the growing emphasis on home life, child-care workers saw no need to keep these mothers and children together. This attitude would persist well into the 1960s.

For a time there were also corrupt brokers who did a brisk black-market business in newborns. Men and women operating "baby farms" preyed on

Orphans of varying ages had their picture taken in the nursery of the Odd Fellows orphans' home, Mason City, Iowa, in 1918.

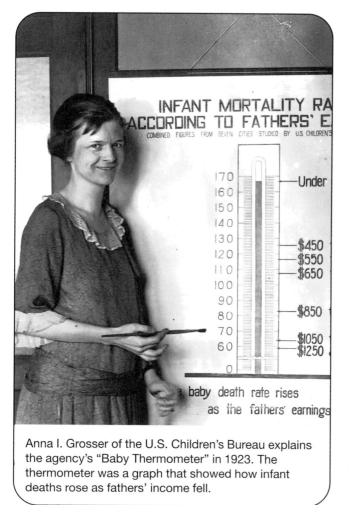

INFANT MORTALITY RA[TE]
ACCORDING TO FATHERS' E[ARNINGS]
COMBINED FIGURES FROM SEVEN CITIES STUDIED BY U.S. CHILDREN'S [BUREAU]

170 — Under
160
150
140
130 — $450
120 — $550
110 — $650
100
90
80 — $850
70
60 — $1050
— $1250
0

[th]e baby death rate rises
as the fathers' earnings

Anna I. Grosser of the U.S. Children's Bureau explains
the agency's "Baby Thermometer" in 1923. The
thermometer was a graph that showed how infant
deaths rose as fathers' income fell.

desperate single mothers and sold infants to adoptive parents for as little as twenty-five dollars, with no questions asked. Hastings Hart of the Russell Sage Foundation, an organization formed in 1907 to conduct social research, reported that one woman obtained a baby for "25 cents and a canary bird. . . ."

Like others at the 1909 conference, Hart believed that young people raised in asylums led "an artificial life." In large institutions, Hart explained, "the bell rings for [children] to get up, to say their prayers, to go to breakfast, to school and to play, and back from play." He explained what this meant to a child: "It means that some one else is doing his thinking for him; some one else is planning his life for him; he does not develop initiative; he does not develop spontaneity; and he goes out at the age of fifteen or sixteen handicapped." Hart was convinced that children needed to live in a home with a family if they were to grow up normally.

The document written at the 1909 conference called for the creation of a federal agency to oversee the welfare of all young Americans. At the time, Congress was considering legislation that would create just such an agency. After three years of planning and debate, Congress passed a bill establishing the U.S. Children's Bureau, and on April 9, 1912, President William Howard Taft signed the bill into law. The mission of the Children's Bureau was to gather facts and report on topics ranging from infant mortality to juvenile delinquency.

At the end of the 1909 conference President Roosevelt had called the experts' recommendations "not only important for the welfare of the children immediately concerned, but important as setting an example of a high standard of child protection by the National Government. . . ." Asylum managers, in contrast, saw the conference report as an attack, and they responded by changing the way they operated. Now they tried even harder to create a homelike atmosphere. Many asylums began to employ the cottage system that had been used for years at the Massachusetts Industrial School for Girls and other places. The children in these institutions lived in clusters of houses, called cottages, rather than in one big, forbidding building.

Orphans now went out regularly to picnics, fairs, and circuses. Some returned home to spend vacations and holidays with their families. Asylums also relaxed their rules: In the 1920s, for example, the Chicago Nursery and Half-Orphan Asylum began to let children talk during meals.

Change came more quickly to some asylums than to others, though. The Hebrew National Orphan Home, where Sammy Arcus grew up in the 1930s, remained large and strictly regulated. "We marched to everything—the synagogue, the dining hall—without talking," Arcus remembered. Discipline was harsh at the asylum, and at times children were abused, physically and sexually, by staff members and older boys. Arcus himself lost his teeth as a young man because of damage done years earlier, when he was beaten by a supervisor.

With great fanfare, New York City orphans take off on an automobile outing. This photograph was taken in front of City Hall in 1906.

Despite the harsh aspects of life in the home, "Most of us led fairly happy lives," said Ira Greenberg, who lived in the asylum with Sam Arcus. "We were busy growing up," Greenberg added, "and no matter how bad things got for us, they were made more bearable by our knowing that we were all in this together."

The home sponsored clubs for boys interested in photography, stamp collecting, dramatics, and other activities. Sam Arcus joined all but the Rod and Gun Club, and he served as president of most. Through that experience, he said, "I learned that I was smarter than I thought I was."

Today, Yonkers, New York, has an urban look, but when Sam Arcus was a child, it was in the country. He and his friends hiked for miles in the fresh air, something they never could have done in the city. They raided the asylum's apple orchard so early in summer and so often that the fruit never

In the twentieth century, asylum children took an active part in American life. These Rochester, New York, orphans plant a vegetable garden as part of a nationwide effort to grow and conserve food during World War I.

had a chance to ripen. They grew up among horses, goats, chickens, and dogs. The boys played baseball and other sports on the home's athletic fields and rode the swings on its playground. The clear sky and open spaces enriched the children's lives, but the hours-long journey from the neighborhoods they'd left made it hard for parents to visit.

In the 1930s Arcus and other asylum children had enough food to eat and warm clothes to wear. Meanwhile, outside institution walls thousands of young Americans went without milk and fresh vegetables. These children wore threadbare clothing and listened as their parents worried aloud about money. The Great Depression, the worst period of economic hardship in U.S. history, had arrived.

No single event caused the Great Depression, but the catastrophe that marked its start was the stock-market crash of October 29, 1929. Stock prices had reached dizzying highs because of risky, unchecked trading. Then they began a rapid and dangerous fall. Millions of people who had invested in the market saw their holdings—and their hopes—wiped out. Banks closed in the wake of the stock-market crash, and families lost their savings. Businesses folded, and millions of American workers were suddenly without jobs. In 1933, at the height of the Depression, one-fourth of the workforce was unemployed.

As during earlier economic downturns, many parents coped by placing children in asylums. Although child-care experts had favored home placement ever since the 1909 conference, the number of American children living in institutions reached a high of 150,000 in 1933. The frustrated manager of a Kentucky asylum reported that "there are two children sleeping in every single bed, and some are sleeping on the floor." Young people also remained in asylums longer, since the practice of placing children as apprentices or indentured servants had ended. A growing number of young Americans, including those in orphanages, waited to start working until they had finished high school.

Free foster homes were becoming a thing of the past. In 1909, when

In 1935 residents of the Hebrew National Orphan Home presented the operetta *H.M.S. Pinafore*. Because the home was a boys' asylum, boys played the female roles.

the child-care professionals met in the nation's capital, a large part of the U.S. population still lived on farms. Rural families often took in a child to raise without expecting financial help, because the child's work on the farm was well worth the cost of his or her board. But by the 1930s many Americans had left farms and moved to cities and suburbs. With the Depression straining household budgets, few families could afford to give a home to a child without financial support. Most of the 249,000 children living in foster care in 1933 lived with families who received money from the state for the children's care.

The number of children needing care was rising at a faster rate than the number of families wiling to take them in. As a result, even with orphan asylums and the foster-care system stretching their resources to help, thousands of girls and boys remained homeless. Some were adolescents, mostly boys, who had left home to give their parents one less mouth to feed. They wandered the country, stealing rides on freight trains. "I hugged my mom and told her I'd keep in touch," said Jim Pearson, who left Newton, North Carolina, in 1931, when he was thirteen. "I didn't want to leave, but felt I had no choice."

Many more homeless young people came from the drought-stricken Southwest, which became known as the Dust Bowl. The states of Oklahoma, Texas, Kansas, New Mexico, and Colorado were hardest hit by a long drought that began in 1931. Without rain, crops withered and died. Strong winds raised great clouds of dry soil and carried them eastward for miles before dropping them to earth in great drifts.

Orphaned and needy children from the tenements of Manhattan enjoy a hayride at the Salvation Army's home for destitute children in Spring Valley, New York.

Unable to make a living off the land, hundreds of thousands of people packed their belongings into old cars and trucks and fled the region. Most went to California, hoping to find work picking peaches, lettuce, and other crops in the large West Coast agricultural industry. All too often they found disappointment instead, with too many workers competing for a limited number of jobs. For countless Dust Bowl refugees, home was a camp by the side of a road or a cardboard shack in one of the shantytowns known as Little Oklahomas. Children became sick easily and often in the crowded, unsanitary camps.

The Depression forced so many hardworking Americans to live hand-to-mouth that people could no longer blame poverty on character flaws. Following the inauguration of President Franklin D. Roosevelt in 1933, the federal government passed a series of laws to aid needy citizens and spark the economy. Known collectively as the New Deal, these laws protected banks, boosted the prices paid to farmers for their crops, and put people to work. Under one piece of New Deal legislation, the Social Security Act of 1935, the government began providing Aid to Dependent Children (later called Aid to Families with Dependent Children). Working through state agencies, the U.S. government gave financial help to children in their own homes.

The Social Security Act was good for children but bad for orphanages. Private asylums were already coping with reduced contributions as a result of the Depression. Once tax dollars

A father visits his sons at the Jewish Orphan Home of Cleveland, circa 1912.

An Oklahoma farmer and his family, refugees from the Dust Bowl, stand beside their stalled car in the California desert. The children in this family were among the thousands of young Americans made homeless by the Great Depression.

went to support poor children, people gave even less. Asylum managers short of funds watched helplessly as buildings fell into disrepair. Roofs leaked and went on leaking; cracked windows let in drafts all winter long. Many institutions never recovered.

Social Security and other forms of public aid also helped adults remain at home and out of poorhouses. As states and counties built institutions to care for the mentally ill and the disabled, poorhouses either closed their doors for good or evolved into nursing homes for the aged poor.

Many reformatories also closed in the first decades of the twentieth century. The idea that young people guilty of crimes should be locked up to serve their sentence had fallen out of favor. For one thing, houses of refuge, like orphan asylums, required children to grow up in an institution rather than in the natural setting of home and family. For another, there were concerns that children sentenced to reformatories would be branded as criminals for life; as adults they might be barred from good jobs because they never would gain an employer's trust. And worse, children themselves would come to believe that they were bad. The commissioner of the New York State Board of Charities noted that the grated windows, high walls, and massive doors of the reformatory "tend to break down pride of character and self-respect. The boy under such circumstances must feel that the world has turned its back upon him; that he has lost all; that every man's hand is against him, and that henceforth he must be against every man."

The states created juvenile courts to handle cases involving children age sixteen or younger. Instead of punishing children for breaking the law, the judges of the juvenile courts searched for the reasons underlying a child's behavior. They addressed problems in the health, family life, and education of each child who came before them and frequently placed young offenders under the watchful eye of a probation officer. Then as now, this professional on the court staff worked with wayward children to prevent their mistakes from being repeated. The public was willing to let minors go free with supervision but preferred to see adult offenders punished. In 1878 Massachusetts became the first state to pass a probation law for juveniles. The first adult probation law was passed in New York more than twenty years later, in 1901. By 1956 all states had both juvenile and adult probation laws.

Laws in many states became more lenient toward young offenders in other ways. According to a New York statute of 1905, all crimes committed by children younger than sixteen, except crimes punishable by death or life in prison, were considered misdemeanors. (People of the twenty-first century are often surprised to learn that before 1900, at least ten children in the United States under fourteen were sentenced to death and executed for murder, rape, arson, or other crimes.) In 1909 the New York legisla-

Judge Benjamin Barr Lindsey of the Denver Juvenile Court praises past offenders who have learned to obey the law. This photograph was taken between 1920 and 1925.

ture changed the law so that children under sixteen would be guilty not of misdemeanors but of juvenile delinquency. And after World War II New York created a new category, Persons in Need of Supervision (PINS), for youth with serious behavior problems who came to the attention of the juvenile justice system. These were young people who do not attend school as required by law, abuse drugs or alcohol, act violently, run away, or are too disobedient for their parents or guardians to control. Other states soon followed New York's example.

World War II ended in 1945, when the United States and its allies defeated first Germany and then Japan. Americans enjoyed prosperity in the postwar years, but orphan asylums continued to lose support. A few still housed dependent children, but many had closed. Most that remained open had evolved into agencies that helped young people with special needs. In 1927 the Washington City Orphan Asylum had become the Hillcrest Children's Center, a residence for youngsters needing psychiatric

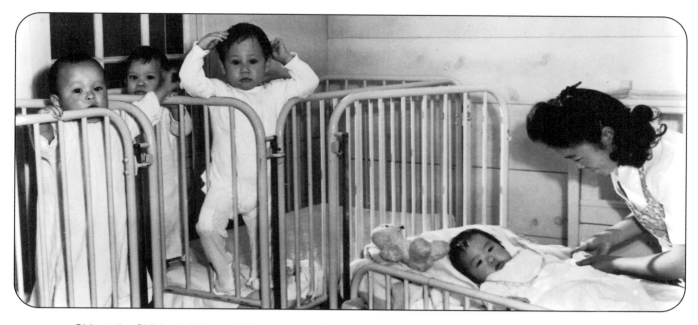

Girls at the Children's Village at Manzanar, a relocation camp for Japanese Americans located two hundred miles northeast of Los Angeles. As part of its effort to confine Americans of Japanese ancestry during World War II, the U.S. government imprisoned about one hundred orphans and foster children, some as young as six months of age.

care. Similarly, in the mid-1940s the New York Colored Orphan Asylum changed its name to the Riverdale Children's Association and began to offer family counseling.

Nevertheless, by 1961 about 82,500 American children were still being cared for in orphanages. Twice as many were in foster care. By 1977 the number of children in orphanages had dropped to 43,000, but the number in foster care had swelled to 394,000.

The tremendous increase in foster care had followed the publication in 1962 of an important article in the *Journal of the American Medical Association*. Titled "The Battered-Child Syndrome," the article described young children brought to hospital emergency rooms with broken bones, head injuries, and other signs of trauma that could have been inflicted only by a parent or guardian. The most serious attacks resulted in permanent brain injury or even death. More often, however, battered children returned to the hospital again and again, each time with new fractures or wounds. Parents' explanations for the injuries failed to account for their seriousness.

Too often in these cases, according to the authors, physicians hesitated to inform the proper authorities. The authors wrote, "Temporary placement with relatives or in a well-supervised foster home is often indicated to prevent further tragic injury or death." The article was only eight pages long, but it had a huge impact. Doctors throughout the United States read it and followed its recommendations.

But the resulting heavy reliance on foster care alarmed members of Congress and pushed them to pass the Adoption Assistance and Child Welfare Act of 1980. This law required children needing help or care to live in the most familylike setting available. With the goal of keeping children in their own homes, the law provided money for programs to address poverty, domestic violence, drug and alcohol abuse, and other problems

Residents of the Hillcrest Children's Center in Washington, D.C., make their beds and prepare for the day on a morning in 1947.

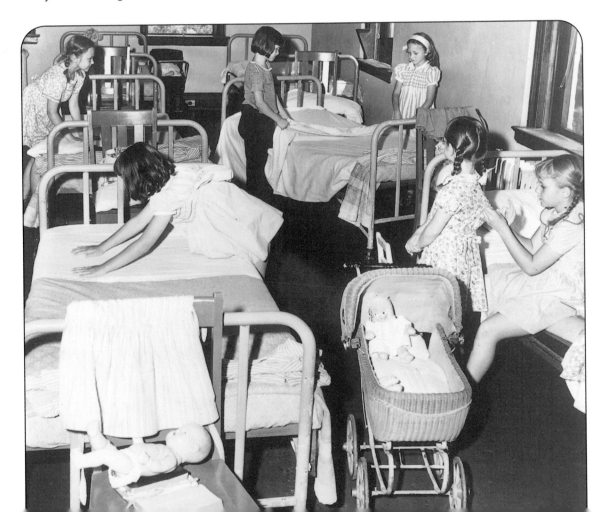

that stressed families. The law made funds available to encourage the adoption of older children and children with physical or mental disabilities. It also stipulated that children in foster care were to be reunited with their families as quickly as possible. With the government so strongly committed to family care, nearly all the existing orphanages closed.

Did the 1980 act achieve what Congress had set out to accomplish? If asked, many Americans would have answered, No. By the late twentieth century the public was concerned that society's problems had come to resemble those of the 1800s. There was a growing gap in income, with the rich getting richer and the poor growing poorer. Teenage boys in the nation's inner cities, unable to find jobs, were joining gangs, abusing drugs, and committing violent crimes. Many children were counted among the homeless, often because their parents were unemployed, earned too little money to pay rent, or received too little public assistance. In one year, 1986, more than thirteen thousand children spent time in New York City's shelters for the homeless. Most of these children were in single-parent families headed by women. Meanwhile, some people raised a complaint that was often heard in the nineteenth century and never proved, that welfare destroys the desire to work.

Searching for solutions, some people discussed bringing back orphanages. In 1994 the speaker of the House of Representatives, Newt Gingrich, created a furor when he backed a bill that would have let states use federal money to create orphanages for children of women receiving welfare. That bill never became law. Meanwhile, the courts began sentencing young offenders to military style "boot camps" to discourage them from committing more crimes. For many people the strict discipline of these camps recalled the harshness of houses of refuge.

In 1999 about 547,000 American children were in foster care, and 117,000 of those children were waiting to be adopted. Increasingly, youngsters enter foster care after being abused or neglected. Many have parents who are dependent on drugs or alcohol, and some of the young

Victor Jackson grew up in the Dorsey Home for Dependent Colored Children, an asylum that opened in Rochester, New York, in 1910. He later became recreational supervisor for the City of Rochester.

people themselves were born addicted to drugs. The children's resulting behavior problems, coupled with a shortage of foster homes, have led to a system in which youngsters move repeatedly from one home to another. Also, some foster homes fail to meet basic standards. Although foster parents undergo screening and training, there have been instances of abuse in their homes. About ten percent of foster children are physically abused by the adults caring for them. In one study twenty-four percent of girls and eight percent of boys reported disturbing sexual contact while in foster care. And, all too often, those reunited with their parents return to foster care when problems at home recur.

It may be that society needs to find new and varied ways to help children who require substitute care. "There is no one-size-fits-all solution," cautions Sam Arcus, himself an aging orphan. He advises keeping an open mind and asking, "What are the needs of this particular child?"

 Sam Arcus *(right)* with his wife, Adele, and
their children, Norman and Shelly, in 1982.

AFTERWORD

❧

Where Life Led Some of the Children Who Appeared in This Book

Sam Arcus remained at the Hebrew National Orphan Home through high school. After graduating in 1940, he held a variety of jobs, from garment cutter to vacuum-cleaner repairman. He began to study at the City College of New York (CCNY) in 1942, while working at the Pride of Judea Children's Home, a Jewish orphanage. He earned a degree in sociology from CCNY in June 1947 and a master's degree in social work from Columbia University in February 1949. Arcus, his wife, Adele, and their two children lived in cities throughout the United States while he pursued a career in social work with the Young Men's Hebrew Association (YMHA), Young Men's Christian Association (YMCA), and Jewish community centers. Sam Arcus has written a memoir, short stories, and other works inspired by his stay at the Hebrew

National Orphan Home. In 2004, at the age of eighty-two, he was still active professionally with the Pima Council on Aging in Arizona. He is listed in the 2003 and 2004 editions of *Who's Who in America*.

George Gallarno lived in the Iowa Soldiers' Orphans Home at Cedar Falls until he was sixteen. He became a civil servant, working in the Office of the Auditor in the Iowa State House in Des Moines. In the 1890s he served as president of the Soldiers' Orphans Home Association, an organization of adults who had lived as children in Iowa's homes for Civil War orphans. (When the home at Cedar Falls closed in 1876, the staff took everything, including furniture, records, and any photographs of the orphans that might have existed.)

Alice Humiston, one of the three "mystery" soldier's orphans of the Civil War, never married. As an adult she moved from town to town in New England and New York and tried several careers, including chicken farming. She ended her days in southern California, living with a daughter of her brother Frank. She died in 1933, at age seventy-six, when her skirt touched a heater and caught fire.

Frank Humiston graduated from Dartmouth College in Hanover, New Hampshire, and the University of Pennsylvania's School of Medicine in Philadelphia. He settled in Jaffrey, New Hampshire, and was a country doctor. He and his wife had six children. Frank Humiston died in 1912, following surgery to remove gallstones. He was fifty-seven.

Fred Humiston earned his living selling grain. His work took him up and down the Atlantic seaboard, from Canada to Florida. He had a wife and two daughters, and made his home in West Somerset, Massachusetts. He died of heart disease in 1918, at fifty-nine.

John Jackson, the boy placed with a cruel master by the Philadelphia House of Refuge, became a ship's cabin boy following his escape. He sailed to such exotic places as New Orleans and Spain before coming ashore in New York and moving into the Newsboys' Lodging House. On January 26, 1859, he was among a group of children who left New York by train with a representative of the Children's Aid Society. In Pawpaw, Indiana, a farmer selected John and took him home. John left the farm a year later, but he remained in the area for the next few months. He joined the Union army once the Civil War began and was wounded at the Battle of Shiloh, fought in Tennessee on April 6 and 7, 1862. John Jackson died of his wounds in June 1863, at the age of eighteen.

Mary Ellen Wilson lived a long and useful life. Following the trial of the Connollys, Mary Ellen went to live with the sister of Etta Wheeler, the charity worker who brought her case to the attention of Henry Bergh. She later married a man named Lewis Schutt and had two daughters, both of whom grew up to be teachers. Mary Ellen Schutt appeared on behalf of organizations dedicated to helping children. She died in 1956, when she was ninety-two years old.

ENDNOTES

❧

All cited books and articles are listed in the bibliography.

CHAPTER 1: THROWN UPON THE WORLD

p. 1   Barber, "The Orphan Home, the Orphan Home . . ." is from "The Orphans' Welcome," in Solenberger, p. 52.

p. 5   Crockett, "I would rather risque myself . . ." is from Crockett, p. 49.

p. 5   Crockett, "What a miserable place . . ." is from Crockett, p. 50.

p. 7   Hartley, "are content to live in filth . . ." is from *Eighth Annual Report of the New-York Association for Improving the Condition of the Poor*, p. 18.

p. 7   "the vagrant and vicious children . . ." is quoted in *Eighth Annual Report*, p. 18.

p. 7   "They are not left to feel . . ." and "The industrious poor are discouraged . . ." are from Fay, p. 3.

p. 9   "The poor houses throughout the State . . ." is quoted in Axinn and Stern, p. 61.

p. 9   "Common domestic animals . . ." is quoted in Bremner 1974, p. 121.

p. 9   Folks, "The poorhouse became the dumping-ground . . ." is from Folks, "The Child and the Family," in Bremner 1974, p. 119.

p. 10   "Shelter Us Under the Shadow . . ." is quoted in Sharlitt, p. 19.

p. 11   "The din of the city . . ." is quoted in Black, p. 13.

p. 11   "well-placed and elegant ladies" is from "Summary of the History of the Washington City Orphan Asylum," p. 1.

p. 11   "little ones who seem to have been thrown . . ." is from Jenkin Lloyd Jones, p. 6.

p. 12   "instill into the youthful minds . . ." is quoted in Bellows, p. 132.

CHAPTER 2: ASYLUM CHILDREN

p. 16   Greenough, "Mid rank and wealth . . ." is quoted in Peacock, p. 17.

p. 17   "I am a little orphan . . ." is from "I Am a Little Orphan" in Solenberger, p. 51.

p. 22   "within the last twelve months . . ." is from *1840 Annual Report of the Washington City Orphan Asylum*, unnumbered page.

p. 22   "poor-house smell" is from Black, p. 135.

p. 23   "thirteen were suffering . . ." is quoted in Roth, p. 33.

p. 23   Child, "Everything moves by machinery" is quoted in Rothman, p. 229.

p. 23   "From the first of April . . ." is quoted in Axinn and Stern, p. 75.

p. 25   "The children shall be dressed . . ." is quoted in Axinn and Stern, p. 73.

p. 25   "Each day shall begin . . ." is quoted in Morton, p. 11.

p. 27   "might be better" is quoted in Bellows, p. 140.

p. 27   "There are now five classes . . ." is quoted in Black, p. 28.

p. 27   "reading, writing, spelling . . ." and "having all the characteristics . . ." are quoted in Hacsi, p. 176.

p. 28   "We have recently been able to dispense . . ." is from *1860–61 Annual Report of the Washington City Orphan Asylum,* unnumbered page.

p. 29   "Many have been the boys . . ." is from *Moral Recreations, in Prose and Verse,* p. 7.

p. 29   "The first symptom of real grief . . ." is from *Moral Recreations, in Prose and Verse,* p. 14.

p. 31   "placed in a situation . . ." is from *1841 Annual Report of the Washington City Orphan Asylum,* unnumbered page.

p. 31   "suitable to his or her condition . . ." and "to see that the terms . . ." are from *Revised Statutes of the State of Illinois,* p. 53.

CHAPTER 3: SAVING YOUTHFUL HEARTS

p. 33   "Some of them merest children yet . . ." is from "The Boys' Cell," p. 471.

p. 33   "vicious tempers and habits" is quoted in Rothman, p. 215.

p. 34   Stanford, "crocodiles in human shape" is from Stanford, p. 11.

p. 34   Stanford, "[W]ith extended jaws . . ." and "What generous soul . . ." are from Stanford, p. 13.

p. 35   Maxwell, "Many notorious thieves . . ." is quoted in Griscom, p. 181.

p. 35   "Unless the heart is corrupt . . ." is quoted in Hawes, p. 28.

p. 35   Maxwell, "The most depraved boys . . ." is quoted in Peirce, p. 79.

p. 36   Stanford, "hospitable dwelling . . ." is from Stanford, p. 22.

p. 36   "We would take the pliant spirit . . ." is from Mayer, pp. 7–8.

p. 36   Dickens, "an odd, and, one would think . . ." and "to reclaim the youthful criminal . . ." are from Dickens, p. 49.

p. 38   Abdy, "It was painful to observe . . ." is quoted in Holloran, p. 141.

p. 38   "heinous crime of seduction . . ." is quoted in Hawes, p. 50.

p. 39   Devoe, "It would be no great piece . . ." and "Each room should also be provided . . ." are from Devoe, p. 48.

p. 40   Devoe, "Some complain that it is too relaxing . . ." is from Devoe, p. 46.

p. 41   Devoe, "I asked an intelligent boy . . ." is from Devoe, p. 48.

p. 41   Curtis, "does not obey the orders . . ." is quoted in Rothman, p. 232.

p. 41   Curtis, "I do not believe . . ." is quoted in Sedgwick, p. 102.

p. 41   Peirce, "To this day . . ." is from Peirce, p. 77.

p. 41   "the best behaved . . ." and "very vicious and disobedient," are from Teeters, p. 173.

p. 42   "excluded almost entirely . . ." is quoted in Rothman, p. 230.

p. 42   Devoe, "would go about the yard . . ." is from Devoe, p. 64.

p. 42   "little prisoners" and "The great throng . . ." are quoted in Teeters, p. 174.

p. 43   Curtis, "large notorious & hardened villains" and "I fear that . . . introducing . . ." are quoted in Hawes, p. 43.

p. 43   Stanford, "degree of Bachelor of Arts in crime" is from Stanford, p. 11.

p. 43   "has absented herself from home . . ." and "made the acquaintance of a bad girl . . ." are quoted in Brenzel, p. 120.

p. 46   "and of others . . ." is quoted in Bremner 1980, p. 173.

p. 47   "We have parted with a large number . . ." is quoted in Mennel, p. 22.

CHAPTER 4: LET SOCIETY BEWARE!

p. 49   "His father and mother are wicked and bad . . ." is from Horwood, p. 8.

p. 50   "She was clothed in a filthy, tattered gown . . ." is from French, p. 607.

p. 50   Brace, "My observation has been . . ." is quoted in O'Connor, p. 158.

p. 50   Brace, "The asylum system is . . ." is from Brace, p. 77.

p. 51   Brace, "Let society beware . . ." is quoted in Bremner 1980, p. 88.

p. 51   Brace, "city missionary," is quoted in O'Connor, p. 72.

p. 51   Brace, "Her husband had fever and ague . . ." is from *Third Annual Report of the Children's Aid Society*, p. 27.

p. 52   Brace, "the immense number of boys and girls . . ." is quoted in Hawes, p. 91.

p. 52   Brace, "The habits and passions of the street boy or girl . . ." is quoted in Hawes and Hiner, p. 129.

p. 53   Brace, "God's reformatory" is quoted in Hawes, p. 88.

p. 53   Smith, "little ones of Christ" is quoted in O'Connor, p. xv.

p. 54   "My friends want children . . ." is quoted in Bremner 1980, p. 87.

p. 56   "too poor to support him," "son of a poor man . . ." and "broken down laborer" are quoted in Mandler, p. 133.

p. 56   "I think that I like the country . . ." and "I am getting along first rate . . ." are from *Fourth Annual Report of the Children's Aid Society*, pp. 46–47.

p. 57   "She is a very bad girl . . ." is from *Fourth Annual Report*, p. 51.

p. 58   "vicious character" is from *Laws Relating to Interstate Placement of Dependent Children*, unnumbered page.

p. 59   "doubtful characters" is from 1860 Federal Census, NARA Microfilm Series: M653, Roll 789, Book 1, Fourth Ward, Division Two.

p. 63   Brace, "treat the lads as independent little dealers . . ." is quoted in Hawes, p. 96.

CHAPTER 5: SOLDIERS' ORPHANS

p. 65   Porter, "'My father fell on the field of blood . . .'" is from "The House of Mercy," in Solenberger, p. 55.

p. 68   "He has finished his work on earth . . ." and "Of what inestimable value . . ." are from "Whose Father Was He?," p. 4.

p. 70   Lincoln, "bind up the nation's wounds . . ." is from "Second Inaugural Address" in Banis, p. 147.

p. 70   Johnson, "take up the destitute orphans . . ." and "a solid moral basis . . ." are quoted in Harrsch, p. 85.

p. 71   "respected men and fathers . . ." is quoted in Ragan, p. v.

p. 73   Burrowes, "reasonable degree of silence . . ." and "wholesome, sufficient, and regular food" are quoted in Paul, pp. 100–101.

p. 73   Dankoler, "several times punished . . ." and "laughing was thrashed out of me" are quoted in Harrsch, p. 101.

p. 73   Gallarno, "was a man of fiery red hair . . ." and "accounted for his sternness . . ." are from Gallarno, p. 171.

p. 74   Gallarno, "What battles my mother fought . . ." is from Gallarno, p. 169.

p. 74   Gallarno, "Those Saturday afternoon holidays . . ." is from Gallarno, p. 179.

p. 76   Gallarno, "In the town of Cedar Falls . . ." is from Gallarno, p. 176.

p. 78   "nothing but ragged pants to wear . . ." is quoted in Bremner 1980, p. 102.

p. 80   "The Adopted Children of Wisconsin" is quoted in Harrsch, p. 104.

p. 81   "The general conviction in this community . . ." is quoted in Dunkelman, p. 2.

p. 81   Gallarno, "Sometimes the children at the Home . . ." is from Gallarno, pp. 192–93.

CHAPTER 6: EVERYBODY'S BUSINESS

p. 83   Loyle, "Unknown, ideal, unseen mother . . ." is from Loyle, p. 163.

p. 83   "mould the entire future . . ." and "by doing their utmost . . ." are from Farrar, pp. 101–102.

p. 84   "The buildings are in such miserable repair . . ." is quoted in Reynolds, p. 15.

p. 85   Riis, "Home, the greatest factor . . ." is from Riis, p. 119.

p. 86   Lowell, "How to care for the children . . ." is from Lowell, p. 72.

p. 86   "He was crying bitterly . . ." is from *First Annual Report of the Board of State Charities,* p. 35.

p. 86   "unless such child be an unteachable idiot . . ." is quoted in Axinn and Stern, p. 105.

p. 88   "What is everybody's business . . ." is from Dudley, p. 99.

p. 90   Riis, "I saw a child brought in . . ." is quoted in Harlow, p. 153.

p. 90   Bergh, "The child is an animal . . ." is quoted in Harlow, p. 154.

p. 90   Wilson, "I am never allowed to play . . ." is quoted in White, p. 215.

p. 91   Bergh, "the poor, dumb animals . . ." is quoted in Harlow, p. 151.

p. 91   Dudley, "[The father's] defense . . ." is from Dudley, p. 106.

p. 95   "kind mother to all . . ." is quoted in Solenberger, p. 60.

p. 95   "excessively delicate organization . . ." is from Abbott, p. 17.

p. 95   "If the parent or teacher has tact . . ." is from Abbott, pp. 79–80.

p. 95   "the matron appeals to their sense . . ." is quoted in Hacsi, p. 156.

p. 97   "faced immediate indenture . . ." is quoted in Hacsi, p. 157.

p. 97   Coit, "The superior development of one member . . ." is from Coit, pp. 11–12.

CHAPTER 7: THIS ARMY OF CHILDREN

p. 101   Johnson, "Oh, when I am grown . . ." is from "Day Dreams," in Harvey, p. 26.

p. 101   Roosevelt, "The interests of the nation are involved . . ." is from *Proceedings of the Conference on the Care of Dependent Children,* p. 5.

p. 101   "Home life is the highest and finest product . . ." is from *Proceedings of the Conference,* p. 5.

p. 102   "Homeless and neglected children . . ." is from *Proceedings of the Conference,* p. 6.

p. 104   Hart, "25 cents and a canary bird . . ." is from Hart, p. 229.

p. 104   Hart, "an artificial life," "the bell rings for [children] to get up . . ." and "It means that some one else . . ." are quoted in Bremner 1974, p. 467.

p. 105   Roosevelt, "not only important for the welfare . . ." is from *Proceedings of the Conference,* p. 8.

p. 106   Greenberg, "Most of us led fairly happy lives" and "We were busy growing up . . ." are from Greenberg, p. 5.

p. 107   "there are two children sleeping . . ." is quoted in Marshall B. Jones, p. 624.

p. 109   Pearson, "I hugged my mom . . ." is quoted in Uys, p. 56.

p. 112   "tend to break down pride of character . . ." is from Letchworth, p. 25.

p. 115   "Temporary placement with relatives . . ." is from Kempe et al., p. 24.

SELECTED BIBLIOGRAPHY

Abbott, Jacob. *Gentle Measures in the Management and Training of the Young, or, the Principles on Which a Firm Parental Authority May Be Established and Maintained.* New York: Harper & Brothers, 1899.

Axinn, June, and Mark J. Stern. *Social Welfare: A History of the American Response to Need.* 5th ed. Boston: Allyn and Bacon, 2001.

Banis, Robert J., ed. *Inaugural Addresses: Presidents of the United States from George Washington to 2008.* 2nd ed. Chesterfield, Mo.: Science and Humanities Press, 2001.

Bellows, Barbara L. *Benevolence Among Slaveholders: Assisting the Poor in Charleston, 1670–1860.* Baton Rouge, La.: Louisiana State University Press, 1993.

Black, Robert L. *The Cincinnati Orphan Asylum.* n.p.: Robert L. Black, 1952.

"The Boys' Cell." *Harper's Weekly,* July 23, 1870, p. 471.

Brace, Charles Loring. *The Dangerous Classes of New York, and Twenty Years' Work Among Them.* New York: Wynkoop & Hallenbeck, 1880.

Bremner, Robert H. *The Public Good: Philanthropy and Welfare in the Civil War Era.* New York: Alfred A. Knopf, 1980.

———, ed. *Care of Dependent Children in the Late Nineteenth and Early Twentieth Centuries.* New York: Arno Press, 1974.

Brenzel, Barbara M. *Daughters of the State: A Social Portrait of the First Reform School for Girls in North America, 1856–1905.* Cambridge, Mass.: MIT Press, 1983.

Cmiel, Kenneth. *A Home of Another Kind: One Chicago Orphanage and the Tangle of Child Welfare.* Chicago: University of Chicago Press, 1995.

Coit, Stanton. *Neighbourhood Guilds: An Instrument of Social Reform.* London: Swann Sonnenschein and Co., 1891.

Crockett, Davy. *An Account of Col. Crockett's Tour to the North and Down East.* Philadelphia: E. L. Carey and A. Hart, 1835.

Devoe, Elijah. *The Refuge System, or Prison Discipline Applied to Juvenile Delinquents.* New York: John R. M'Gown, 1848.

Dickens, Charles. *American Notes: A Journey.* New York: Fromm International, 1985 (first published in 1842).

Dudley, Oscar L. "Saving the Children: Sixteen Years' Work among the Dependent Youth of Chicago," in *History of Child Saving in the United States.* By the National Conference on Social Welfare, Committee on the History of Child-Saving Work. Montclair, N.J.: Patterson Smith, 1971.

Dunkelman, Mark H. "Key to a Mystery." Military.com. URL: http://www.military.com/Content/MoreContent1/?file=cvw_g_mystery. Downloaded on September 16, 2003.

1840 Annual Report of the Washington City Orphan Asylum. n.p., Hillcrest Children's Center Collection, Library of Congress.

1841 Annual Report of the Washington City Orphan Asylum. n.p., Hillcrest Children's Center Collection, Library of Congress.

1860–61 Annual Report of the Washington City Orphan Asylum. n.p., Hillcrest Children's Center Collection, Library of Congress.

Eighth Annual Report of the New-York Association for Improving the Condition of the Poor. New York: John F. Trow, 1851.

Farrar, Frederic William. *Woman's Work in the Home as Daughter, as Wife, and as Mother.* Philadelphia: Henry Altemus, 1895.

Fay, Joseph Dewey. *Pauperism: To the Citizens of Philadelphia, Paying Poor Taxes.* Philadelphia: Privately published, 1827.

First Annual Report of the Board of State Charities, to the Governor of the State of Ohio, for the Year 1867. Columbus, Oh.: L. D. Myers & Bro., 1868.

Folks, Homer. *The Care of Destitute, Neglected, and Delinquent Children.* Albany, N.Y.: J. B. Lyon Co., 1900.

Fourth Annual Report of the Children's Aid Society. New York: J. P. Prall, 1857.

French, Fanny S. "The Beggar Child and Church." *Ladies' Repository,* October 1858, p. 607.

Gallarno, George. "How Iowa Cared for Orphans of Her Soldiers of the Civil War." *Annals of Iowa,* January 1926, pp. 163–93.

Greenberg, Ira A., ed. *The Hebrew National Orphan Home: Memories of Orphanage Life.* Westport, Conn.: Bergin & Garvey, 2001.

Griscom, John H. *Memoir of John Griscom, LL.D. . . .* New York: Robert Carter and Brothers, 1859.

Hacsi, Timothy A. *Second Home: Orphan Asylums and Poor Families in America.* Cambridge, Mass.: Harvard University Press, 1997.

Harlow, Alvin F. *Henry Bergh: Founder of the A.S.P.C.A.* New York: Julian Messner, 1957.

Harrsch, Patricia G. "'This Noble Monument': The Story of the Soldiers' Orphans' Home." *Wisconsin History,* Winter 1992–1993, pp. 82–120.

Hart, Hastings H. *Preventive Treatment of Neglected Children.* New York: Arno Press, 1971.

Harvey, Gail, ed. *Poems of Childhood.* New York: Avenel Books, 1989.

Hawes, Joseph M. *Children in Urban Society.* New York: Oxford University Press, 1971.

———, and N. Ray Hiner, eds. *American Childhood: A Research Guide and Historical Handbook.* Westport, Conn.: Greenwood Press, 1985.

Holloran, Peter C. *Boston's Wayward Children: Social Services for Homeless Children, 1830–1930.* Rutherford, N.J.: Fairleigh Dickinson University Press, 1989.

Holt, Marilyn Irvin. *The Orphan Trains: Placing Out in America.* Lincoln, Neb.: University of Nebraska Press, 1992.

Horwood, Miss. *The Deserted Boy, or, Cruel Parents.* Philadelphia: William Charles, 1817.

Jones, Jenkin Lloyd. *Not Institutions but Homes.* Chicago: All Souls Church, 1893.

Jones, Marshall B. "Crisis of the American Orphanage, 1931–1940." *Social Service Review,* December 1989, pp. 613–29.

Kempe, C. Henry, M.D.; Frederic N. Silverman, M.D.; Brandt F. Steele, M.D.; William Droegemueller, M.D.; and Henry K. Silver, M.D. "The Battered-Child Syndrome." *Journal of the American Medical Association,* July 7, 1962, pp. 17–24.

Laws Relating to Interstate Placement of Dependent Children. By the Children's Bureau of the United States. Washington, D.C.: Government Printing Office, 1924.

Letchworth, William P. *Homes of Homeless Children.* New York: Arno Press, 1974 (reprint of the 1903 edition).

Lowell, Josephine Shaw. *Public Relief and Private Charity.* New York: G. P. Putnam's Sons, 1884.

Loyle, Lonnie. *Neath the Shadow of His Wing.* Clinton, S.C.: Thornwell Orphanage Press, 1900.

Mandler, Peter, ed. *The Uses of Charity: The Poor on Relief in the Nineteenth-Century Metropolis*. Philadelphia: University of Pennsylvania Press, 1990.

Mayer, Charles F. *Laying of the Corner Stone of the Baltimore House of Refuge: and the Address upon the Occasion*. Baltimore: James Lucas, 1852.

McCausland, Clare L. *Children of Circumstance: A History of the First 125 Years (1849–1974) of Chicago Child Care Society*. Chicago: R. R. Donnelly and Sons, 1976.

Mennel, Robert M. *Thorns & Thistles: Juvenile Delinquents in the United States, 1825–1940*. Hanover, N.H.: University Press of New England, 1973.

Moral Recreations, in Prose and Verse. London: Hodgson & Co., 1800.

Morton, Marian J. "Homes for Poverty's Children: Cleveland's Orphanages, 1851–1933." *Ohio History*, Winter-Spring 1989, pp. 5–22.

O'Connor, Stephen. *Orphan Trains: The Story of Charles Loring Brace and the Children He Saved and Failed*. Boston: Houghton Mifflin, 2001.

Patrick, Michael D., and Evelyn Goodrich Trickel. *Orphan Trains to Missouri*. Columbia, Mo.: University of Missouri Press, 1997.

Paul, James Laughery. *Pennsylvania's Soldiers' Orphan Schools*. Philadelphia: Claxton, Remsen & Haffelfinger, 1876.

Peirce, Bradford Kinney. *A Half Century with Juvenile Delinquents: The New York House of Refuge and Its Times*. Montclair, N.J.: Patterson Smith, 1969 (first published in 1869).

Proceedings of the Conference on the Care of Dependent Children, Held at Washington, D.C., January 25, 26, 1909. Washington, D.C.: Government Printing Office, 1909.

Ragan, Diane, comp. *Soldiers' Orphan Schools of Western Pennsylvania*. Pittsburgh: Western Pennsylvania Genealogical Society, 1999.

Revised Statutes of the State of Illinois. Springfield, Ill.: William Walters, 1845.

Reynolds, Marcus T. *The Housing of the Poor in American Cities: The Prize Essay of the American Economic Association for 1892*. College Park, Md.: McGrath Publishing Co., 1969.

Riis, Jacob. *How the Other Half Lives*. Cambridge, Mass.: Belknap Press, 1970.

Rosenberg, Charles E. *The Cholera Years: The United States in 1832, 1849, and 1866*. Chicago: University of Chicago Press, 1962.

Roth, Francis Xavier. *History of St. Vincent's Orphan Asylum, Tacony, Philadelphia*. Philadelphia: "Nord-Amerika" Press, 1934.

Rothman, David J. *The Discovery of the Asylum: Social Order and Disorder in the New Republic*. Boston: Little, Brown and Co., 1990.

Sedgwick, C. M. *Memoir of Joseph Curtis, a Model Man*. New York: Harper & Brothers, 1858.

Sharlitt, Michael. *As I Remember: The Home in My Heart*. Privately published, 1959.

Solenberger, Willard E. *One Hundred Years of Child Care in New Haven: The Story of the New Haven Orphan Asylum and the Children's Community Center, 1833–1933*. New Haven, Conn.: Children's Community Center of the New Haven Orphan Asylum, 1933.

Stanford, John. *A Discourse on Opening the New Building in the House of Refuge, New-York*. New York: Mahlon Day, 1826.

"Summary of the History of the Washington City Orphan Asylum." n.d., Hillcrest Children's Center Collection, Library of Congress.

Teeters, Negley K. "The Early Days of the Philadelphia House of Refuge." *Pennsylvania History*, April 1960, pp. 165–187.

Third Annual Report of the Children's Aid Society. New York: M. B. Wynkoop, 1856.

Uys, Errol Lincoln. *Riding the Rails: Teenagers on the Move During the Great Depression*. New York: TV Books, 2000.

White, Frank Marshall. "The Epoch of the Child." *Outlook*, May 28, 1910, pp. 214–25.

"Whose Father Was He?" *The Philadelphia Inquirer*, October 19, 1863, p. 4.

PICTURE CREDITS

꙳

INDEX

꒰꒱

Note: Page numbers in **boldface** indicate illustrations.